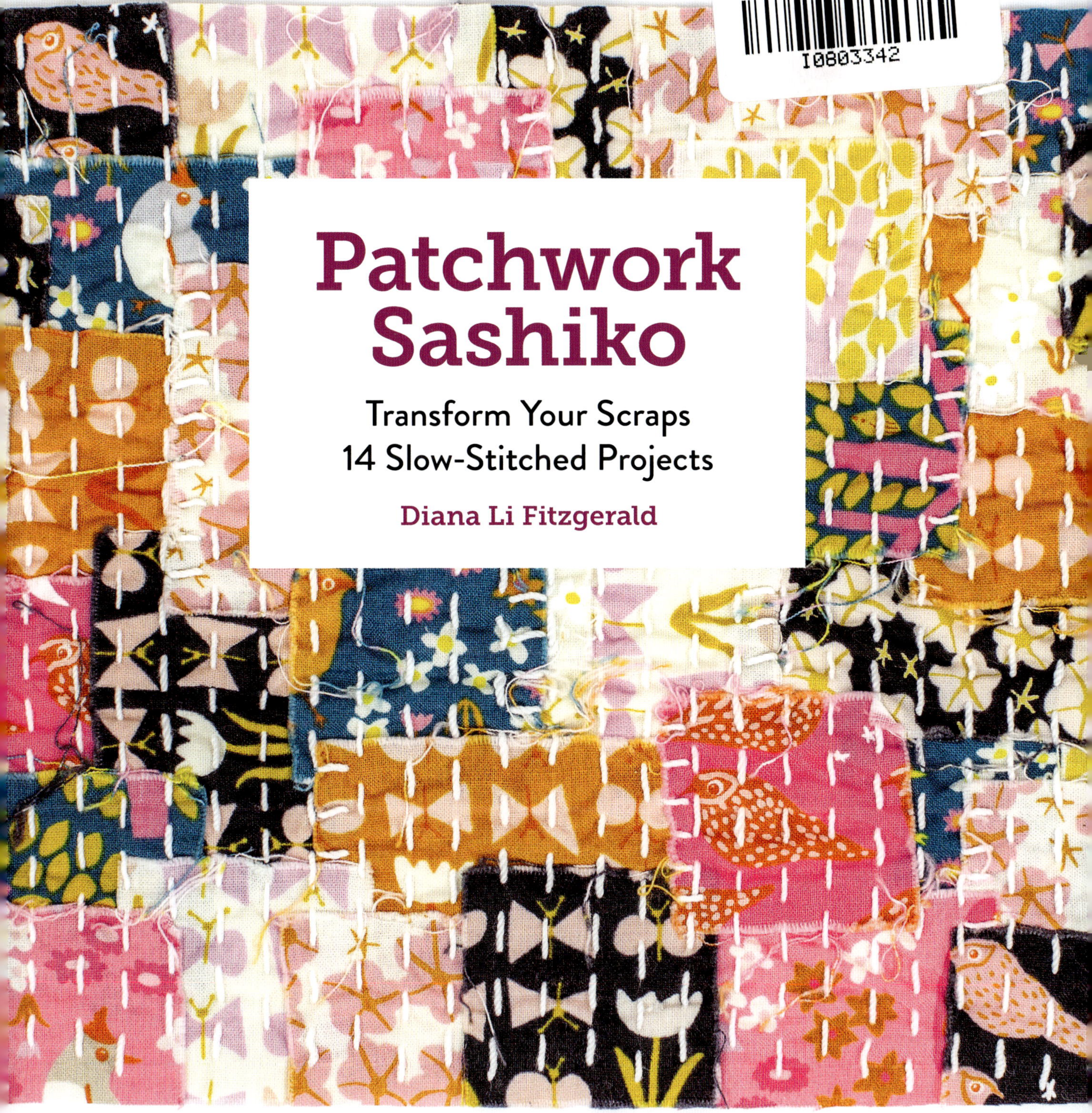

Patchwork Sashiko

Transform Your Scraps
14 Slow-Stitched Projects

Diana Li Fitzgerald

stashBOOKS®
an imprint of C&T Publishing

Publisher: Amy Barrett-Daffin

Creative Director: Gailen Runge

Senior Editor: Roxane Cerda

Editor: Madison Moore

Technical Editor: Helen Frost

Cover/Book Designer: April Mostek

Production Coordinator: Zinnia Heinzmann

Illustrator: Kirstie Pettersen

Front cover photography by Clara Wang Photography

Lifestyle photography by Clara Wang Photography; instructional photography by Diana Li Fitzgerald, unless otherwise noted

Published by Stash Books, an imprint of C&T Publishing, Inc., P.O. Box 1456, Lafayette, CA 94549

Library of Congress Control Number: 2025024678

Printed in the USA

10 9 8 7 6 5 4 3 2

Dedication

To Jonathan, you'll always be in my top 10.

Acknowledgments

My family and friends have been constant cheerleaders that help me believe that what I'm doing is worthwhile. I am grateful to the countless number of people in the sewing and crafting industry that have taken time to encourage me to keep going. And all my wonderful customers who have unwittingly provided motivation for me to keep creating. I am thankful for the staff at C&T Publishing, especially Roxane Cerda, Madison Moore, and Helen Frost, who have shown nothing but patience and dedication to helping this first time author figure it out!

CONTENTS

INTRODUCTION TO PATCHWORK SASHIKO

The slow-stitching traditions we're familiar with today—like Boro, Sashiko, and Kantha—began centuries ago across different parts of the world. These techniques use a combination of hand stitching, scraps of fabric, and design traditions going back hundreds of years. But they all share a distinctive look: A smattering of colors and prints held together with hand stitching that draws you in. It's hard to describe why we're attracted to the effect. Perhaps it's how fleeting the moment feels—these textiles capture a moment of existence with the help of some strategically placed threads.

The Patchwork Sashiko Method combines different elements that define these long-standing and beautiful traditions. It features raw-edged fabric scraps held together with a running stitch that extends through a base layer of lightweight fabric. The result is a stable and pliable textile ready to live its second life.

Patchwork Sashiko textile

Influences and Other Handwork Traditions

I like to experiment when I develop sewing projects. Combining techniques and pulling in methods from different disciplines is what I love most about sewing! All the traditions I am describing here contain elements that I find fascinating and beautiful. My hope is that Patchwork Sashiko encapsulates a bit of the spirit of each of these techniques. Let's look at each one and what makes it unique.

Photo by Irina Lankina/Shutterstock.com

Boro

It is generally accepted that Boro originated during the 17th century in Japan. The practice was created out of necessity to mend and extend the life of garments. The result is a style that is practical and beautiful at once. Today, Boro patches may be strategically placed to create an aesthetically pleasing design, but the original primary purpose was to patch holes and reinforce the cloth of a worn garment.

Photo by Nichola Chapman/Shutterstock.com

Kantha

South Asian regions of India and Bangladesh gave rise to Kantha more than a thousand years ago. It is a practice of giving new life to old and discarded fabric by layering them and applying a running stitch throughout to provide strength. The fabric pieces are usually much larger than with Boro and the fabric edges are not raw. Old saris in an array of colors become soft over time and are layered to create a well-used Kantha stitched blanket or pillow. Today, it is common to find kantha cloth—many pieces that have been simplified into a single layer of fabric with the same Kantha style running stitch in multiple colors.

Photo by Lora Sutyagina/Shutterstock.com

Sashiko

It is hard to separate the traditions of Sashiko and Boro because they are intertwined through history. Sashiko began as straight running stitches applied to strengthen Boro patchwork. Today, Sashiko stitching is typically applied to a single layer of indigo fabric in intricate decorative geometric designs using white thread. The look is distinctive and much more rigid than the Boro or Kantha stitching aesthetic.

Example of Kawandi by Sujata Shah

Kawandi

Kawandi uses small pieces or strips of fabric to assemble a quilt top. Similar to Kantha, Kawandi originated with the Siddi community in India as a way to repurpose old cloth into a new, useful item. But, in Kawandi, the fabric is placed in a particular arrangement. The small pieces are layered around the backing of the quilt, starting from the outside perimeter and working toward the center. Fabric edges are turned under and stitched down with a running stitch, so no raw edges are visible.

Patchwork Sashiko

At the beginning of all my workshops, I briefly explain that I am not an expert in any of the specific traditions I just described. When I began making Patchwork Sashiko pieces, I had the very specific goal of developing a method that would create a stable, pliable textile that also appeared delicate enough that it could fall apart at any minute!

I love the raw edges of Boro that form through years of mending tears and holes. I am drawn to the uniformity and clean texture of Sashiko stitching. The variable patchwork nature of Kawandi deeply inspires what I create, but without the turned edges. I use straight, running stitches to bind together multiple pieces of fabric, like in Kantha, though my scraps are much smaller. I also use exclusively white thread (across many colors of fabric) and small stitches, akin to Sashiko. Patchwork Sashiko is a continuation of all these traditions.

It is no surprise that separate cultures at separate times developed their own means of mending and repurposing their fabrics. It was a necessity to give these textiles an extended life. Today, we can appreciate these techniques for their practicality, beauty, and sustainability.

Patchwork Sashiko has a distinct look, doesn't require specialty tools, and is fully functional. It isn't just an aesthetically pleasing object; it can also be used without fear of it falling apart or fraying to the point of disrepair. There are a few features of a Patchwork Sashiko textile that are unique because of how they come together.

Raw Edges and 'Random' Placement

Placing and arranging the raw-edged fabric scraps is one of my favorite parts of a Patchwork Sashiko textile. Although the layout of the fabric pieces appears random or haphazard, there are defined steps and rules to create this appearance. It is not random that the patchwork appears random! This is a bit of a contradiction that we'll work through together as we start our first textile. All the raw edges are left visible.

Patchwork pieces laid out before stitching

Uniform Hand Stitching

In Patchwork Sashiko, the entire textile is covered with a running stitch (in white thread) that is as uniform in length as possible. As you will see later in the book, the length of the stitches can change depending upon the size of the patchwork pieces. There is an optimal length to achieve a stable textile that becomes smaller or larger corresponding to the size of the patchwork pieces.

Uniform Rows

The uniform-length stitches must also be stitched in uniformly-spaced rows. This gives continuity to the smattering of different colors and patterns of fabric that make up the textile. It lends a cohesive element that allows the eye to see the textile as a whole, instead of just as little fabric pieces. Like the length of the stitches, the row spacing can change depending upon the size of the patchwork pieces.

How to Use this Book

I hope you will use this book as the starting point in your journey to be more creative with what you already have on hand. When we make a quilt, a bag, or a garment, there are a lot of scraps left over. I know I struggle with the drive to create less waste while, at the same time, craving the newest most drool-worthy fabrics! You can do both! With Patchwork Sashiko, you will use every crumb of those coveted fabrics so that they don't just become part of your scrap pile.

This book teaches you to create patchwork pieces from fabric yardage in order to learn the method. You may be wondering why we cut into new fabrics when this method seems so well-suited to using up scraps. The short answer is that the best way to learn is to use the same materials I teach with. Then, once you've mastered the technique, you can apply it to your own scraps.

I developed this method through experimentation, and I encourage you to run your own experiments! However, it's important to know the rules before you break them. Once you start doing so, follow the rules of any well-designed experiment, and change only one variable at a time. This way, you can see exactly how the change has affected the result compared to the previous iteration.

The most common question I get about Patchwork Sashiko textiles is, "These are beautiful, but what am I supposed to do with them?" Anything and everything! The textile, at its core, is just fabric, so you can use it as you would any other fabric. The textile is very stable once finished, and it can be cut into any shape you need. Use it in your favorite purse pattern, apply it as an adornment to a quilt, or incorporate it into a trim for coat pockets. There is no limit to where you might feature it!

You may find yourself protecting the Patchwork Sashiko textile that you create from this book because you spent a lot of time making it. It's true. Slow-stitching is indeed...slow. But I hope you will find even more excitement and satisfaction in incorporating the textile into a new project, where it'll be used and seen. And, when you do finally cut into it, remember to save your scraps! The scraps you have left over from a Patchwork Sashiko piece can also be reused again. You might even find a project later in the book that utilizes these wonderful little pieces (see Projects to Showcase the Patchwork Sashiko Textiles, page 46).

If you've picked up this book, then I already know you like to learn. My hope is that this book will teach you something new, but also help empower you to continue experimenting and stretching your creative boundaries.

TOOLS AND MATERIALS

When I developed the Patchwork Sashiko Method, I wanted to ensure that the tools were easy to find: nothing too fancy or obscure. Most are tools that sewists already have in their sewing space. I am also a big advocate of using what you have instead of feeling like you need to buy the perfect specialty tool. I strongly believe that limiting our resources forces us to be more creative.

Crewel Needle—Size 2

The hand-sewing needle you use needs to be sturdy enough to stitch through multiple layers of fabric. So, I recommend a size 2 crewel needle. They have a larger eye than a typical sewing needle, which is perfect for crochet thread. Size 2 crewel needles are the most common crewel needle found at local crafting/sewing stores. They are also long enough for you to load multiple folds of fabric onto it.

Silicone Needle Pullers ▶

Silicone needle pullers will be your best friend! They are not rigid like a traditional thimble, which helps grip the needle and protect your fingers as you're stitching. You need one for your thumb, and 2 smaller ones for your pointer finger and middle finger.

Crochet Thread—Weight 10 ▶

Crochet thread has a few great qualities that make it perfect for slow-stitching. First, the thread twist is very tight and uniform. Embroidery floss has a less compact thread twist and will unravel easily into individual threads (it's designed to, so you can stitch with single threads!). Second, the texture of crochet thread is a little rougher than traditional Sashiko thread. This less refined style lends itself to the raw look of Patchwork Sashiko. Finally, crochet thread is very easy to find in many different stores (not just crafting stores).

BERNINA

Unbleached Muslin

Muslin is the unsung hero of the Patchwork Sashiko method. This fabric acts as the base for all the patchwork pieces. It's not flashy, but it serves its purpose well. Use a lightweight muslin to avoid adding weight or bulk to the textile. The unbleached color also makes it easy to see if there are bare-spots in the patchwork.

Pellon P44F: One-Sided Fusible Interfacing

This interfacing is fused to the underside of a finished Patchwork Sashiko textile. It ensures that all the stitches stay in place if you decide to cut or trim the textile. It is very lightweight.

Fabric Marking Tools

I use 2 different types of marking tools depending upon the color of the fabric. I use the Clover Chaco Liner in white for very dark fabrics and Frixion Pens for everything else. The Chaco Liner marks are water soluble. The Frixion Pen ink is heat-sensitive and disappears with a quick steam of the iron.

Quilter's Ruler

Quilter's rulers are clear acrylic, so you can see the fabric through it. I suggest a ruler that is 2″ or 3″ wide, and 18″ long. We will use the ruler for drawing lines that are exactly ¼″ apart.

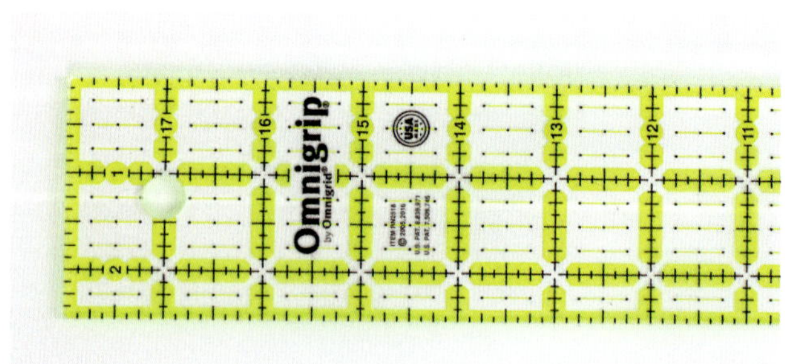

Basic Sewing Tools

You'll also need to keep a few other basic sewing tools on hand for every project. I suggest a sewing machine with an adjustable length straight stitch (for basting and sewing your textiles in a project), an iron and ironing board, fabric scissors, snips, a seam ripper, a stiletto, straight pins, and clips. I prefer to use straight pins that are a little longer than the typical pin, usually labeled as long.

Rotary Cutter

To cut the small, uniformly sized patchwork pieces, I suggest using a rotary cutter and 6″ × 24″ quilting ruler. I generally use a 45mm size blade.

Thread Snips

These are different from fabric scissors, and they make cutting threads fast and easy. They have 2 blades that are spring loaded for quick snipping.

Other Project Interfacings

Most of the projects require additional interfacing, beyond the P44F used in the Patchwork Sashiko Method.

Fusing Interfacing

Lay the fusible side (the rough side) up. Place the fabric WS down on the stabilizer or fleece. Set the iron to the directed setting. Press overlapping areas until the entire piece is fused.

Pellon SF101 Shape-flex: This is a lightweight woven interfacing that is fusible on one side. It gives the fabric a little extra reinforcement and adds very little weight or bulk. Set the iron to high with steam.

Pellon 70 Peltex Sew-In Ultra Firm Stabilizer: This stabilizer is the sturdiest you can get! This version is not fusible and is sewn into the projects.

Bosal In-R-Form Single Sided Fusible Foam Stabilizer: This stabilizer gives a lot of body to bags and is also quiltable. It's soft but supports a rigid shape. Set the iron to high. Mist the entire piece with water before pressing.

Pellon 987F Fusible Fleece: This fleece gives your fabric a light cushion without any stiffness. Set the iron to high with steam.

Patchwork Pieces

The small patchwork pieces are the star of the textile. I suggest using quilting cotton or fabric of similar weight. Quilting cotton is offered in every beautiful color and pattern you can think of!

It is possible to use heavier weight fabrics like corduroy, denim and canvas, but hand stitching through multiple layers with heavier weights is very difficult. Batiks are also not recommended because despite being lighter weight, the weave is dense and more difficult to hand stitch through.

Size

The basic method uses two sizes: 1½″ × 1½″ squares and 1½″ × 2¼″ rectangles. These sizes are optimal for the suggested stitch length when you're hand stitching. Later in the book, we'll discuss scaling up these sizes (see Change it Up!, page 40), but for now, stick to these standard sizes, and use them to calculate how much fabric you need.

Calculating Fabric Usage

Even though you're working with scraps and small pieces, it's important to consider fabric usage. It's often not always necessary to know exact fabric consumption, and each project will recommend how much total fabric you need. But, this section walks you through how to plan fabric usage in case you need it.

Let's start with a simple formula that assumes you're using pieces of fabric that are all the same size. The numbers in parentheses are example dimensions. Multiply the length and width of the finished textile you plan to make (aka the size of the muslin backing):

muslin backing length (7″) × muslin backing width (9″) = 63 square inches

All of the pieces you layer on the muslin backing will overlap with one another, meaning that they will cover less space than their size accounts for. So, double the above number to account for the "extra" space lost to overlapping. So, we need enough patchwork fabric to cover 126 square inches.

Repeat this process with the size of the patchwork pieces. We're using pieces that are 1½″ × 1½″ as an example:

patchwork length (1½″) × patchwork width (1½″) = 2¼ square inches

Divide the area you need to cover by the area of each patchwork piece. This gives the number of patchwork squares needed to cover the muslin space (round up if needed):

muslin area (126″ squared) / patchwork piece area (2¼″ squared) = 56 squares

Finally, divide the above number by the total number of different fabrics you plan to use, which will give us how many square patchwork pieces you need per fabric (again, round up):

number of squares (56) / number of fabrics (12) = 5 patchwork pieces per fabric

I mentioned earlier that you'll be using both squares and rectangles, so your patchwork pieces are more than one size. This changes the math a little bit. The "number of sizes" value in the equation below changes depending upon how many different patchwork piece sizes you are using. In this example, we are using just 2 different sizes.

So, in the above example, if you're using an equal number of pieces of two different sizes, divide 5 by 2 and round up. You need 3 of the square patchwork pieces per fabric.

Repeat each of the above equations for the 1½″ × 2¼″ rectangles:

muslin area (126″ squared) / patchwork piece area (3⅜″ squared) = 37 rectangles
number of rectangles (37) / number of fabrics (12) / number of sizes (2) = 2 patchwork pieces per fabric (rounded up)

So, with this calculation, you'd cut 2 rectangles 1½″ × 2¼″ and 3 squares 1½″ × 1½″ in each of the twelve fabrics to cover a 7″ × 9″ muslin rectangle.

From here, it's easy to determine and cut yardage. You can cut both these shapes from 1½″ × WOF (width of fabric: 40″–44″) strips. So, figure out how many shapes fit in each strip. You can cut 26 squares 1½″ × 1½″ from a WOF strip. You can cut 17 rectangles 1½″ × 2¼″ from a WOF strip. And, you can cut 24 strips 1½″ wide from one yard of fabric. That's a lot of patchwork pieces! Of course, that's why this is so perfect for scraps!

For quick calculations, focus on doubling the area of your finished textile to give you a rough estimate of how much fabric you need. This could also be as simple as laying out all your fabric scraps edge to edge and visually checking that the area is about double the muslin size.

PATCHWORK SASHIKO METHOD BASICS

Are you ready to create your first Patchwork Sashiko textile? This chapter will lead you step by step through the process to make sure your first experience is a success.

MATERIALS

- 7″ × 9″ rectangle of muslin
- 7″ × 9″ rectangle of Pellon P44F interfacing
- 12 strips 1½″ × WOF from 12 different fabrics (1 per fabric)
- Crewel needle, size 2
- Cotton crochet thread, size 10 in white
- Thread snips
- 3 silicone needle pullers
- Fabric pen or pencil
- Quilter's ruler (3″ × 18″)
- Seam ripper
- Sewing machine with top and bobbin thread

CUTTING

From each of the 12 strips, cut:

3 squares 1½″ × 1½″ (total of 36)

2 rectangles 1½″ × 2¼″ (total of 24)

Laying the Patchwork

This is the fun part! Well, it's *all* fun, but laying out the pieces is my favorite part. The patchwork pieces laid in a structured yet haphazard style. It's a visual contradiction: consistent rules that produce a layout that appears random. If the patchwork was created in a truly random manner, it would not be reproducible. Our goal in this section is to learn a method that can be repeated over and over again to yield the same aesthetic results.

Thinking Ahead

But before you start laying things out, there's an important question to ask: What do you plan to use your Patchwork Sashiko textile for? While I suggest making a basic rectangle as instructed in this chapter for your first try, you'll soon want to plan for different kinds of textiles.

The Muslin

The size of the muslin is the size of the final textile. But, the hand stitching can cause the entire textile to shrink slightly, so, I suggest adding 1″ to all sides of your desired dimensions. These added inches will also allow you to trim the textile to the size and shape you need. Then, the area within the 1″ border is your "safe zone". You want the area within the "safe zone" to be large enough to use in your future project. The shape of the muslin does not have to be a square or rectangle. If you are using the textile in a sewing pattern, cut the muslin into the same shape as the pattern template and again, add 1″ to all sides. Make sure to consider the muslin's orientation, too. Mark which side is the top to help in deciding stitch direction later.

The 7″ × 9″ size in this chapter is good for learning the rules and getting used to the technique. The "safe zone" for this finished textile is 5″ × 7″. You can finish it in a day and get some quick satisfaction that will make you want to make larger textiles!

Directional fabric (left); non-directional fabric (right)

Directional Fabrics ▲

It's all fun and games until you forget your fabric is directional! Directional fabrics are those with prints that only appear correct in a specific orientation. Pay attention to how you arrange them.

Direction of the Stitching ▲

The direction of the hand stitching is purely personal preference. But, it is still something to plan ahead for. Think about the finished project and what will be most aesthetically pleasing. Which way do you prefer the hand stitching to go? Up and down, left to right, diagonal? It's up to you. I typically orient my stitching vertically within the finished project.

Follow The Layout Rules

1. All edges of each patchwork piece must be parallel and perpendicular with the edges of the muslin. No angles or tilting.
2. Overlap all patchwork pieces by at least ¼″. This is the minimum! Every piece you put down should overlap with others. It's inevitable that, as you place more and more pieces, the overlap will increase. But, because you have to hand stitch through all the layers, you don't want to overlap too much—stitching through 3–5 layers is much more difficult than 2.
3. Cover the entire muslin with patchwork pieces. The muslin should be completely invisible, as the patchwork pieces are the stars of the show. I encourage you to extend your fabric pieces beyond the edges of the muslin as necessary to ensure everything is covered.
4. Spread out the different fabrics, evenly distributing all the different prints and colors as best you can.

1

2

3

5 Stagger the edges of the patchwork pieces. No edges of the patchwork pieces should align.

Layout

Place the muslin in landscape orientation. Choose any 1 of the 12 fabrics and place 2 pieces on the muslin. Any combination of shapes is fine. Space them 3″–3½″ apart, diagonal from one another. I call these the *origin spots*. The patchwork layout will spread from here.

WHAT ABOUT LARGER TEXTILES? • *On a larger piece of muslin, if you maintain the 3″–3½″ spacing, you'll need more origin spots. For instance, an 8″ × 11″ textile will have 5 origin spots equally spaced about 3″ apart from one another (one in the center and the remaining 4 closer to the corners).*

Begin layering more patchwork pieces. Go through each of the 12 fabric types first before moving on. Use the same number of pieces from each fabric (2, because there are 2 origin spots) and follow the rules (page 21). Distribute one of each fabric around each origin spot. This first layout step is essential to establishing the balanced look of the textile.

// What About Color? //

Sometimes, as is the case with this sample, different fabric designs share colors. In addition to keeping the same fabrics away from each other, also try to keep the same colors separated if possible.

Different fabrics with the same colors

Now that you have used 2 pieces of each fabric, continue by choosing your favorite pieces (no longer needs to be 2 of each fabric), and cover the rest of the muslin. Extend out from the origin spots. At this point, you will start to have tiny gaps of exposed muslin. Place pieces on top or slip them under existing pieces to keep the texture varied (see Troubleshooting Placement, page 25). If there is a particular fabric you have a fondness for, wait to place it until the very end so it is most visible on top of the textile.

There will be some pieces left over. This is a good thing! It's much better to have extra than not enough. I had 9 pieces left over after finishing this patchwork. Take one last look. Most importantly, ensure that all the overlaps are sufficient to cover the muslin. When you hand stitch the layers together, it creates a very cohesive look, so you won't be hung up on the one patchwork piece that's sticking out in your mind.

Finished layout

Troubleshooting Placement

Minimal Movement

There will be times when you wish a piece was scooched just a little bit this way or that way. In these cases, use your fingernail to gently scrape the piece over like you are drawing a short line in the direction you want it to go. This will keep you from picking up the piece and potentially moving everything else in the process.

Slivers of Muslin

You will probably experience laying a piece that seems just a little too small for the space it needs to fill. There's probably enough leeway in the overlap of the pieces around it to make it work without needing another piece. We want to avoid adding another piece just to cover a teensy gap, which makes for unnecessary bulk.

In this example, the gap is between the bird print and the leaf print, so I shift *all* the pieces around the bird print until there's just enough fabric to cover the gap with the ¼″ overlap. Don't pick up the pieces unless you have to!

Gaps in the Muslin

As you get closer to finishing the patchwork, it's natural for there to be bare spots of muslin surrounded by patchwork pieces. You have two options when adding a new piece. Gingerly lift up the edge of a piece to slide another underneath. Or, simply lay it right on top. It may look a little odd at this stage to have a piece that isn't below any others, but I promise that it will not be noticeable after hand stitching.

New piece under an existing piece

New piece on top

Securing the Patchwork

Now that the patchwork is exactly the way you want it, you need to secure the pieces in place so that the textile becomes stable enough for hand stitching (and transportation!).

Pinning

Before basting, secure the textile with long straight pins. How meticulous you want to be is up to you. At minimum, every piece needs to be pinned through at least once. But, if you want to keep all the overlaps in the exact same position, I recommend using more pins. It will not be easy to manipulate pieces that shift while you machine baste in the next step.

Insert the pins in the same direction as the future hand stitching. So, since this piece will have vertical stitching, place the pins vertically, parallel to the short edge of the piece. I find that it's easier to do this with the piece in a portrait orientation.

Start pinning at the edge of the muslin closest to you (across the whole edge), then work toward the opposite edge. Use your non-dominant hand to gently hold pieces in place while inserting the pins through all layers with your dominant hand. Push the pin in, then lift up on the entire pin, keeping it parallel to the table, then push the pin out, avoiding moving the pieces as much as possible.

But, pieces will move! Remember the minimal movement tip and gently shift pieces back into place. It's your job to make sure the pieces maintain the minimum ¼″ overlap and don't tilt or rotate. When you're finished pinning, pick up the textile and shake it! Pieces should not fall off. If they do, put the pieces back in place and pin some more.

Basting

Always sew the basting stitches *perpendicular* to the straight pins.

You can machine baste or hand baste. I always machine baste. It's faster and easier to maneuver through the lawn of pins, and I feel it's more secure. But, the benefit of hand basting is that it can be done anywhere with just needle and thread and the result is similar. After basting, you should be able to pick up your textile and shake it without anything falling off!

2a

2b

BASTING WITH SEWING MACHINE

1 Choose a thread color that contrasts with the fabrics. This will make removing the basting stitches easier later on. Set the stitch length on your machine to the longest setting.

2 Position the textile under the presser foot so the long edges are at the right and left. Sew the first line of basting stitches perpendicular to the pins ¼"–½" away from the right edge. Start at the top edge of the textile and continue sewing to the bottom edge. Go slow and remove the pins as you sew. Backstitch at the beginning and end of each line. There are a lot of finicky edges and corners that will try to fold up while you're sewing, so consider using a stiletto to keep them in place.

3 Reposition the needle back at the starting edge where the first and second row pieces overlap. Continue basting. Sew across the textile, making whatever line shape is needed to secure the pieces. The lines of basting stitches don't have to be straight! The goal is to sew over all the overlaps, keeping the position of the patchwork piece edges secure while you are hand stitching later. So, if you need to change the direction you're sewing, stop the machine with the needle down through the project, bring the presser foot up, pivot the piece, then lower the presser foot and continue basting.

BASTING STITCH LINES • *This step is purely functional and the stitches are temporary. The basting lines do not need to be consistently spaced from each other. Sew as needed to secure the patchwork pieces. Again, pick up your textile and shake it! If nothing falls off or is jostled out of place, you've done a good job!*

3a

3b

3c

4a

4b

4 Continue basting the entire textile, repeating Step 3. Trim all basting thread tails.

Hand Stitching

Drawing Lines

Draw lines perpendicular to the basting stitch lines.

1 Align the edge of the ruler approximately ¼″ to ½″ from the bottom edge of the textile, perpendicular to the basting stitches. Make sure the line is past the edge of the muslin base. The rest of the lines will be based upon this first line, so make sure it's visually parallel and perpendicular to the patchwork piece edges.

2 Use the fabric marking pen or pencil to draw a line using the ruler as a guide.

// Use Multiple Marking Tools // *It's likely that your patchwork will have both light and dark pieces, and the line you drew may not be consistently easy to see. Don't be afraid to use different types/colors of marking pens/pencils depending on the fabric color. I sometimes use both a Frixion pen and a white Chaco Liner in the same drawn line.*

2a

2b

Start Stitching

The Patchwork Sashiko stitching method is quite different from traditional Sashiko. Focus on keeping the textile flat on the surface in front of you. Resist the temptation to pick it up as you sew. Keeping the textile flat will help you visualize the needle aligning with the drawn lines and keep the stitch length consistent. It is also easier to push the needle through multiple layers of fabric with the textile flat. Over time, your hands will gain muscle memory for this kind of stitching, and the process will become easier and more natural. It is worth the time to stitch this way!

HANDEDNESS • *The following instructions are written assuming the stitcher is a right-handed person. If you are left-handed, please reverse all the references to right and left.*

1. Cut an approximately 18″ length of crochet thread. Create a knot at one end and thread the other end through the needle, leaving a 1½″ tail. Place silicone needle pullers on the thumb, pointer, and middle finger of your right hand.
2. Push the needle through the fabric, from back to front, at the right end of the drawn line.
3. Pull the thread through, leaving about a ¼″ length of slack thread on the backside so the knot is not snug to the muslin.

1

2

3

4a

4b

4 Place your left hand on the fabric with your fingers pointing towards the needle and centered over the line. Press down with your pointer and middle fingers so the fabric is taut. Push the needle through the fabric with your right hand, following the drawn line, to create $\frac{3}{16}$"–$\frac{1}{4}$" long stitches spaced $\frac{1}{8}$" apart. This equates to about 4 stitches per inch. Push the needle through multiple layers of fabric to create multiple stitches at once. Don't fret about how many folds you get on the needle: do what is comfortable!

// Stitch Length // *These measurements are approximate, so no need to break out a ruler. Smaller stitches = more stitches = greater stability of your pieces (and more texture)!*

5a

5 Once you have as many folds on the needle as is comfortable, hold the needle upright with your left hand and push all the fabric folds down toward the eye of the needle. Then, hold the needle with your right hand and pull the fabric away with your left.

// Give Your Hand a Rest // *Focus on pulling the fabric away from the needle instead of pulling the needle out of the fabric. The motion is easier on your hands as you stitch through multiple layers. You can even pull just one fold off at a time for the least resistance.*

5b

5c

6a

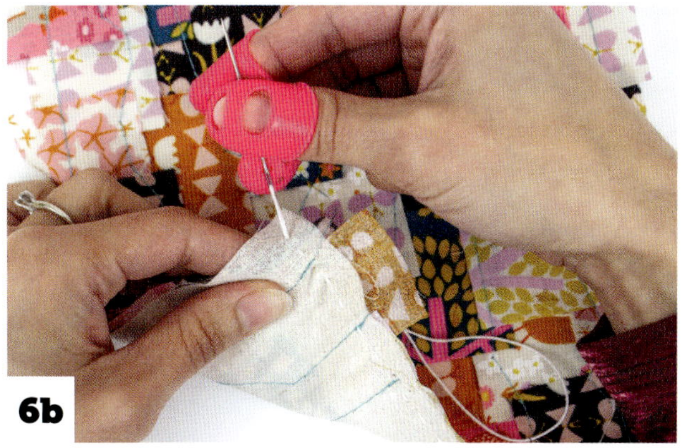

6b

6 Hold the right side of the fabric and smooth it toward the left (in the direction that you are stitching) to reduce puckering. Repeat Steps 4–5 across the entire drawn line, ending with the needle on the backside of the piece.

6c

// Span the Edges // *When you cross the border between two patchwork pieces, adjust the stitch length leading up to the border slightly to ensure that one stitch begins/ends directly before or after each patchwork piece. This will help reduce the amount of additional stitching you may have to do later. If this isn't feasible without sacrificing a generally uniform stitch length, then continue as normal. Additional stitches can be added later to compensate.*

Stitch crossing the edge of a patchwork piece

STITCHES ON THE BACKSIDE • *It's ok if the stitches don't always go through the muslin. As long as the majority of them do, you'll be fine.*

7 Draw the next line *exactly* ¼″ away from the first stitch line and parallel to it.

// Lines and Patchwork Edges // *Sometimes, the drawn lines will align with the edge of a patchwork piece. Hold fast to the line! Do not be tempted to adjust the drawn line to cover an edge, even if your stitches can't be seen. Straight, equidistant lines of stitching are what make the textile visually cohesive.*

ONE LINE AT A TIME • *Over time, as you hand stitch lines into the textile, the entire textile will begin to bow. If you were to draw all the lines at once and follow those lines with the hand stitching, you would end up with stitches that look like a frowny-face or a rainbow as the textile changes! This effect is seen to a greater degree with increased textile size. Even as the fabrics warp, we want the stitch lines to be as straight and parallel to each other as possible, so drawing one line at a time helps achieve this. Starting in the center of the textile and stitching out towards the edges will produce the same effect with curves arcing on both sides of the center line.*

8

10a

8 Turn the textile 180° so you're always stitching from right to left. Repeat Step 2 to insert the needle through the next stitch line, leaving a small thread loop of slack between stitch lines. This slack allows you to make adjustments if you have excessive puckering.

// Curling Thread // *The thread will begin to curl up on itself as you stitch. Simply hold the textile up, let the needle dangle, and the thread will uncurl.*

9 Repeat Steps 4–6. Stop stitching when you have about 3″ of thread left. This doesn't have to be at the end of a stitch line. Make a knot close to the fabric on the backside of the textile and trim the thread.

10 Repeat Steps 1–9, starting new thread where the last stitch ended, until you've stitched the entire patchwork piece.

10b

10c

10d

No-Fail Knotting

I used to struggle with my knots not knotting where I wanted them! Here is a trick that made this much easier: Remove the needle from the thread. Start a loose knot, but don't tighten it yet! Place the tip of the needle through the knot loop, and press the tip against where the thread comes out of the muslin (where you want the knot). Tilt the needle at an angle, and slowly pull the thread tail away from the needle. The knot will slide down the needle and form exactly at the tip of the needle. Magic! Scratch at the knot towards the muslin to tighten it, then snip the tail.

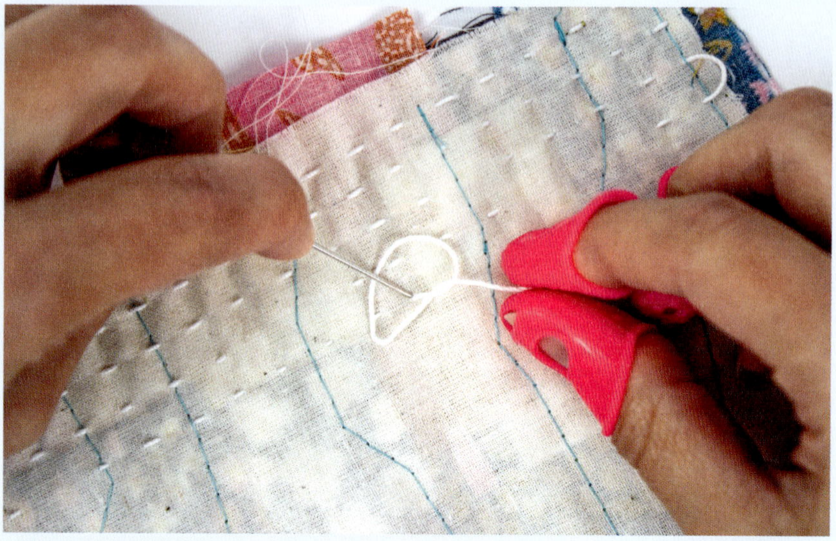

Oh No, a Knot!

If you get an accidental knot in your thread, it's very likely not a *real* knot. These aren't really knots because you can fix them without having to cut the thread and start over. If you get one of these knots, create some slack in the thread around it. Pull hard on the thread on both sides of the knot and voila! It disappears.

Finishing the Textile

Removing Basting Stitches

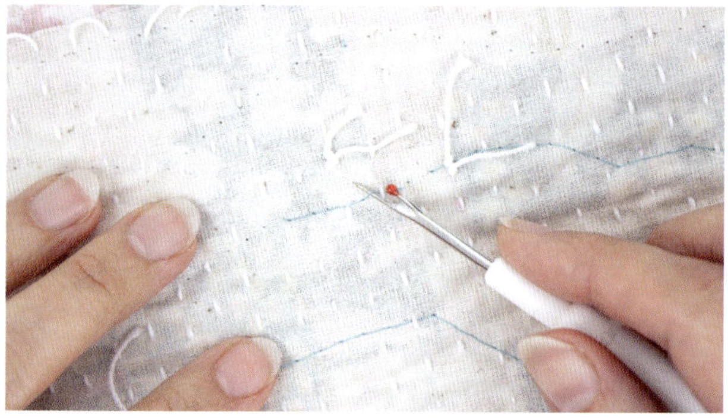

Use a seam ripper to remove all the basting stitches. I like to start from the muslin side and cut every 5–6 stitches or so. Then, scrape the tip of the seam ripper underneath the intact stitches to pull them out. This will release longer lengths of thread at one time instead of cutting smaller pieces of threads. After removing stitches from the back, pull the long lengths of top thread away.

Be careful! Sometimes the hand stitching intersects the basting stitches. If you feel any resistance when removing the basting stitches, pause and carefully inspect to ensure you don't cut through any hand stitching.

Additional Stitching

One of the goals of laying out the patchwork was to cover all the muslin. But we're not perfect. Even when you start out with overlap, sometimes the pieces move a little and expose the muslin or an edge isn't stitched all the way down. The fix is more hand stitching that spans the patchwork edges.

First, mark any exposed muslin with a pin. I like the look of the additional stitching and recommend adding some for texture even if your textile overlaps are perfect!

Pin marking edge needing additional stitching

Secure the loose edges of the patchwork with a visible whipstitch. Bring the needle up from front to back, then refer to the diagram to whipstitch. These additional stitches are perpendicular to the hand-stitched line. Continue until all the loose edges are secure.

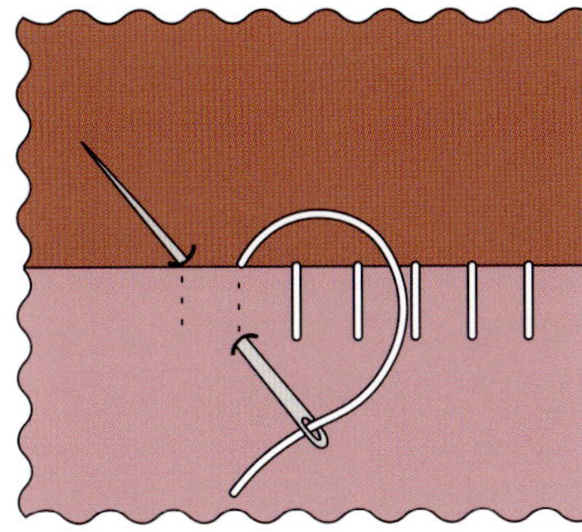

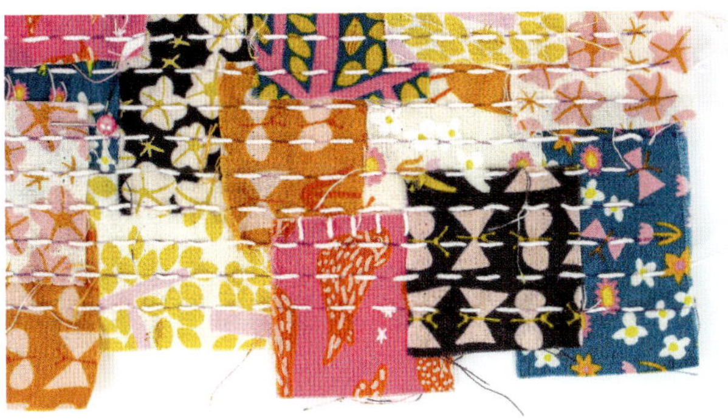

Hand Washing and Double Checking

If you used a Frixion pen, give the textile some steam to remove the marks. Then, use a little soap and handwash the textile. Fold over and gently rub the front together. If you have used a water soluble marking tool, this will remove those marks. We also want the fabrics to shrink, warp, bend—whatever they want to do before you apply interfacing later. After washing, hang or lay flat to dry.

Notice how crinkly and textural the textile becomes after washing and drying? All that crinkliness is going to reveal any exposed muslin we missed the first time. Making sure all muslin is covered ensures that your textile stays consistently raw without sacrificing stability. I frequently find that I've missed at least one spot after the drying process. Apply more additional whipstitching if necessary.

Some stitches will be a little too loose. Or, you may notice some of the stitches are curved resulting from stitching with curled thread. Pull gently on one end of a stitch with a pair of tweezers and continue down the stitch line towards the end. This will eliminate the slack until you reach the end of the line and can pull the thread on the backside. If there is a knot in the middle of the stitch line where you started a new thread length, pull the stitches from that knotted thread towards the closest textile edge to that knot.

Interfacing

The last step is to fuse interfacing to the wrong side of the textile to make sure all stitching stays in place. Before this final step, double-check the textile! When it looks good, gently press the entire textile. Place the textile right side down onto the ironing board or mat. Press any knot tails at the edge of the textile towards the center so they aren't visible from the front side.

Place the Pellon P44F fusible interfacing rough side down on the wrong side of the textile. Trim any interfacing that extends beyond the edges. Set the iron to its high setting with steam. Press down on the fusible interfacing for 6–8 seconds at a time. Lift the iron and move to the next area—do not slide the iron. Continue until the entire piece has been fused. Only press each area once. Flip the textile over to the right side, and press again for 4 seconds at a time. Let cool in place.

Leave it Raw or Trim It Up?

Before we go any further, admire your work! Hold it up to the sunlight; show it to your family and pets! You've worked hard, and I hope your Patchwork Sashiko textile brings a smile to your face. Now, you have a decision to make. The textile can be left raw and mounted into a frame. Hanging your work on the wall makes a beautiful art piece. Or you can trim and cut the textile to use in your next sewing project—in which case, you're in luck since the rest of the book is full of Patchwork Sashiko textile projects!

If you want to trim it, use a pair of fabric scissors or a rotary cutter to cut the textile to the shape you need. This could be based upon your own design or a template provided in your favorite sewing pattern. You've spent a lot of time and effort creating this beautiful textile. So, remember the carpenter's proverb...measure twice, cut once! After cutting, keep those scraps. That scrappy gold can be reused again in other projects!

CHANGE IT UP!

What we've covered so far is the standard way to apply Patchwork Sashiko. But there are so many variations you might be imagining! In this chapter, we'll brainstorm ideas for how to swap this for that and create something totally different.

Scale

You can use larger patchwork pieces to make a Patchwork Sashiko textile. If you do, increase the stitch length and the spacing between stitch rows. This makes sense, right? Imagine if we were to apply larger stitches and row spacing to standard-sized patchwork pieces. There wouldn't be enough stitching to sufficiently secure the fabric to the muslin base. Conversely, using ¼″ stitching and ¼″ stitch line spacing on pieces that are 4″ or larger would be overkill. It would look pretty amazing, but you don't need so much stitching to secure the patchwork. When you scale up, everything scales up.

Larger Patchwork Pieces

There's technically no limit to how much the textiles can be scaled up, but aesthetically, there's an optimal range based on your project. Scaling up for adorning apparel and small upholstery projects doesn't have to be drastic, while if you were making an entire Patchwork Sashiko garment, you may want to take it further.

Use the patchwork piece sizes from the previous section, 1½″ × 2¼″ rectangles and 1½″ × 1½″ squares, as a starting point. Make a visual determination of how large you'd like the squares to be on your project. Let's say, 5″ × 5″ for this example. Calculate the proportional increase in size by finding a scaling-up factor (called the multiplier). Divide the new size by the original size to get the multiplier. Then, multiply the original dimensions of the shape by the multiplier to get the new dimensions of the scaled-up shape.

new square size ÷ original square size = the multiplier
5″ ÷ 1½″ = 3⅓

the multiplier × original rectangle length = new rectangle length
3⅓ × 2¼″ = 7½″

So, the rectangles should be 5″ × 7½″ to proportionately match the 5″ × 5″ squares.

Stitch Length and Spacing

You can use the same multiplier ($3\frac{1}{3}$") to scale up the stitching. Note, that in this case, the calculations are more of a guideline that should be used as the maximum value. You can always go smaller, but going larger may compromise the stability of the textile. The standard stitch length and row spaces are both $\frac{1}{4}$".

original stitch length (or row spacing) × multiplier = new stitch length (or new row spacing)
$\frac{1}{4}$" × $3\frac{1}{3}$ =.83" (rounded up to $\frac{7}{8}$")

So, the maximum stitch length and space between rows is $\frac{7}{8}$" for this scaled-up textile.

Using a multiplier is a great way to start, but consider how the project will be used. Perhaps it will not be handled frequently or is just hung for display. In these cases, increasing stitch length and row spacing beyond these calculations may not be an issue. And it will save you time!

Thread

When the textile is scaled up, the project could also benefit from thicker thread. The weight 10 crochet thread would not have the same impact on a textile three times the standard size.

At a trade show, I decided to drape the top of my booth with a scaled-up textile that could be easily seen by attendees. The thread I used was…medium weight yarn! Use a needle with a larger eye, but avoid really thick needles, as they'll make it harder to stitch through multiple layers.

Design

You may have noticed that while the patchwork pieces in my textiles change, the thread type and color stay the same. Just because I stick with the look of white thread doesn't mean you have to! There's no limit to the kinds of thread weights and colors. Weight 10 crochet thread now comes in an array of beautiful colors. You can also be quite intentional about your patchwork choices!

Go Monochromatic

I love this look. This idea is two-fold. Use the same color fabrics (or the same fabric!) for the patchwork and use a matching thread. Using same color fabrics will still give you some variety of print in addition to providing the raw edged texture. Using patchwork pieces of all the same fabric is striking and is all about the texture. Try using solid fabrics for a very modern look.

Increase Contrast

Contrast doesn't have to scream at you—but it also can! This could be subtle, using neutrals and lighter shades, or a color combination that can be seen a mile away. You can also use more than one thread color.

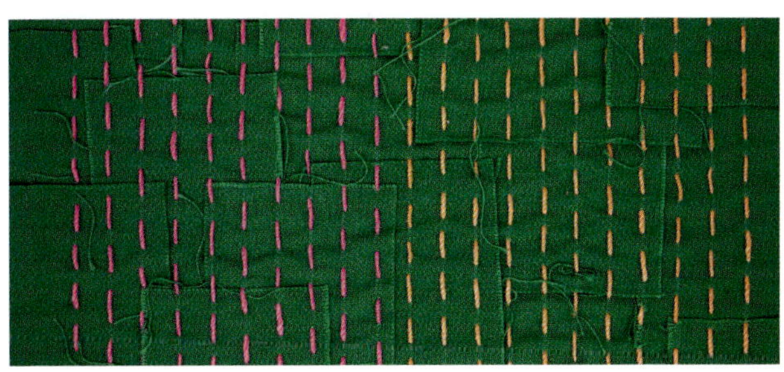

PROJECTS

to Showcase Patchwork Sashiko Textiles

All the projects shown here are designed to showcase the Patchwork Sashiko textile, or use the method in unique and creative ways. If you decide to use a favorite fabric instead of the multi-layered textile, consider using a similarly thick fabric or adding additional interfacing.

For every project, refer to Basic Sewing Tools (page 15) for all the standard tools you'll need. When you cut out project pieces, I recommend labeling them. You can write the piece name directly on the fabric with a fabric pen or pencil, or pin a small piece of paper to the fabric.

Templates

Access the required templates as directed by scanning this QR code or going to **tinyurl.com/11614-patterns-download**

Keep in Mind!

1 Always use a ¼″ seam allowance. I suggest using a ¼″ presser foot to get the most accurate seam allowances. Topstitch ⅛″ from the edge. Baste (outside of the actual Patchwork Sashiko textile) at ⅛″ or less from the edge. Right sides together (RST) and wrong sides together (WST) are abbreviated throughout. (Or, just RS and WS for right and wrong side).

2 Don't be a hero, just pin it! Pinning sufficiently will help keep your sewing accurate.

3 Pressing is the difference between a beautiful handmade project that makes your heart skip a beat and one that's just so-so. Take time to press your seams and your final project.

4 If possible, set your sewing machine to always stop sewing with the needle down (or do this manually). Adjust fabrics and check alignment with the needle throughout each project for security and straight lines.

5 All of the projects that require a zipper suggest a standard presser foot instead of a zipper foot. To effectively install them, move the needle to the left-most position, then position the left edge of the presser foot against the right edge of the zipper teeth.

6 Some of the projects involve quilting. A presser foot seam guide can allow you to skip drawing quilting lines and still get even and precise stitching. If you decide to use this optional tool, look for one that fits your machine.

7 Access the required templates by going to scanning the QR code. Prepare the templates by printing them and then cutting them out of the paper. If you want to make a more long-lasting template, trace the templates onto Pellon 70 Peltex.

Three Stones Tote

FINISHED SIZE: 14″ × 16″ × 3½″

This is no ordinary tote! This project is great for Patchwork Sashiko scraps leftover from a previous project. The shape of the tote is a little narrower and longer than a typical tote bag, and there's an inner zippered pocket. This project reveals my fondness for appliqué circles on half-square triangle blocks!

MATERIALS

- 5½″ × 15½″ interfaced Patchwork Sashiko textile with stitching parallel to long edges
- 5″ × 5″ charm pack squares of quilting cotton in 6 prints or colors
- ¾ yard cotton-linen blend fabric or 100% cotton twill (for bag exterior)
- ⅔ yard of lining fabric (for lining)
- 9″ zipper, size #3 (for inside pocket)
- ¼ yard Pellon SF101 Shape-flex
- ¼ yard Pellon 70 Peltex
- Crewel needle, size 2
- Three Stones Templates 1 and 2

Note on Materials

Make sure to choose quilting cottons that coordinate aesthetically with your Patchwork Sashiko textile! You'll use them to create half-square triangles for the background of the appliquéd circles.

CUTTING LIST

Access the required templates by going to Templates (page 46). Template 1 is a 4″ diameter circle, and Template 2 is a 3″ diameter circle.

For the Appliqué:

Cut 3 squares 4½″ × 4½″ from Pellon SF101 Shape-flex.

Cut 1 of Three Stones Template 1 from Peltex.

Cut 1 of Three Stones Template 2 from Peltex.

Cut 3 squares 4½″ × 4½″ from the Patchwork Sashiko textile.

Bag Exterior

From the bag exterior fabric:

A: Cut 1 rectangle 3½″ × 18½″

B: Cut 1 rectangle 7½″ × 18½″

C: Cut 1 rectangle 2½″ × 4½″

D: Cut 1 square 4½″ × 4½″

E: Cut 1 rectangle 14½″ × 18½″

F: Cut 2 strips 1½″ × 14½″

Handles: Cut 2 strips 4″ × 26″

Lining

From the bag lining fabric:

G: Cut 1 square 7½″ × 7½″

H: Cut 1 rectangle 7½″ × 14¾″

I: Cut 1 rectangle 7½″ × 8″

J: Cut 1 rectangle 7½″ × 3½″

K: Cut 2 rectangles 4″ × 17½″

L: Cut 1 rectangle 14½″ × 18½″

Appliqué Blocks

ORIENTING THE HSTS • *Before completing Step 1, decide your preferred orientation and fabric pairings based on stitch direction, color, and prints.*

1 Pair 2 of the 5″ squares RST, and draw a diagonal line from corner to corner on one piece. Sew ¼″ away from the line on both sides of the line, then cut on the line. Press the seam toward the darker fabric to complete the half-square triangle (HST). Repeat with the other 2 pairs of 5″ squares. Set aside 3 of the 6 HSTs (you won't use them).

2 Place Three Stones Template 1 on the WS of one of the Patchwork Sashiko squares. Trace the template, and cut out the circle. Repeat for the other two squares.

1a

1b

1c

Half-square triangles made from charm pack squares

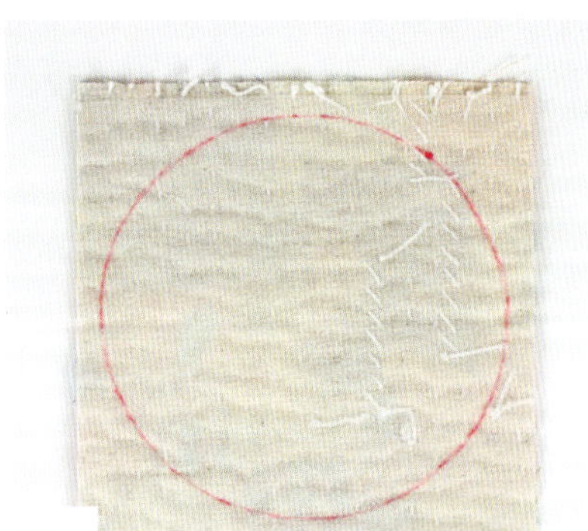

2a

2b

3

4a

4b

4c

4d

3 Cut a 36″ length of sewing thread, and thread the crewel needle. Pull the thread through so it's doubled (18″ in length), and knot the ends together. Sew a running stitch around the perimeter of the circle, ¼″ from the edge and with a ¼″ stitch length. A longer stitch will result in a circle with a less smooth curve. Sew on the WS of the circle, and start with the needle going RS to WS (knot is on the RS). End the last stitch on the RS of the circle.

4 Place the Template 2 Peltex on the WS of the Step 3 circle. Gently pull on the needle, cinching the edges of the circle around the Peltex. Once the curve looks tight and round, tie a knot. Press the appliqué circle with the Peltex still inside; first with steam, then without steam. Remove the Peltex from the appliqué circle, and press again. Repeat Steps 3–4 for the other 2 Patchwork Sashiko circles.

1

3a

3b

4a

4b

Hand Appliqué

1. Center each appliqué circle on the RS of an HST.
2. Pin the circles to the blocks. Thread the needle with another 36″ length of thread (doubled and knotted).
3. To begin a ladder stitch, insert the needle from WS to RS through one HST directly below the folded edge of the appliqué circle. Pull the thread all the way through. Insert the needle in and out through the first layer of the fold, right above where you came up through the HST. The stitch should be ¼″ long.
4. Pull up on the thread to locate exactly where the thread came out of the circle. Using this point as a reference, sew back down through the HST, in and out through the layer of fabric in a ¼″ stitch length.

5 Repeat Steps 3–4 to sew all the way around the circle. After the final stitch, push the needle to the WS of the HST. Knot by making a small stitch within the appliqué circle on the WS. Then, with the needle still in the fabric, wrap the thread around the tip 3 times. Hold the thread in place, and pull the needle through the fabric, tightening the thread. Trim the tail.

6 Repeat Steps 3–5 for the other 2 HSTs and circles.

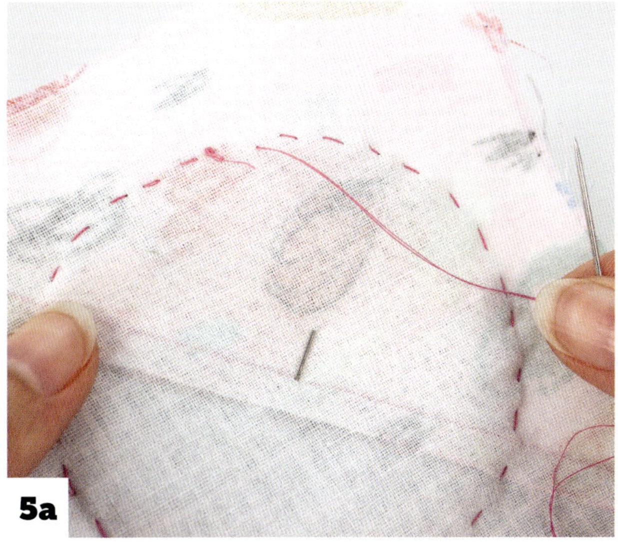

5a

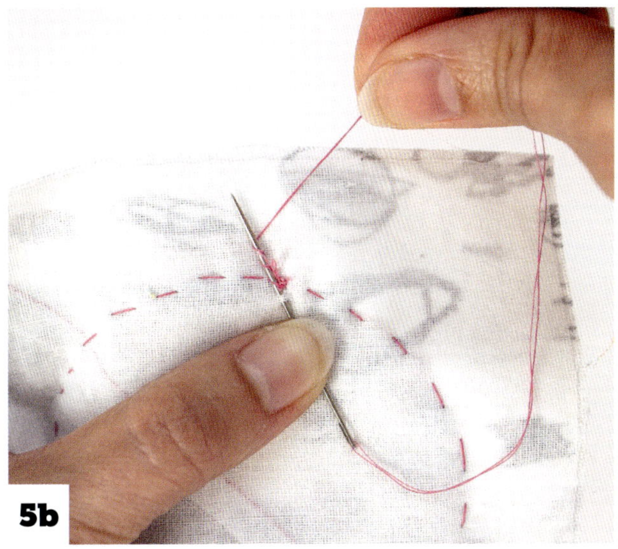

5b

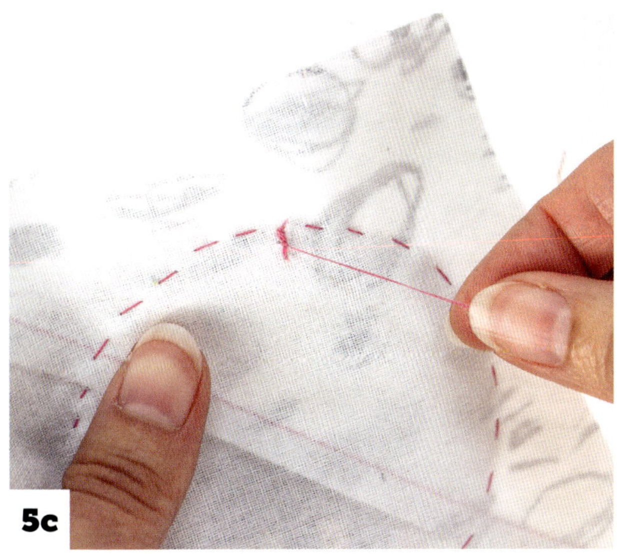

5c

Finish the Blocks

Arrange the appliqué circle blocks in a row. Sew them together on the sewing machine with a ¼″ seam allowance to create the appliqué Strip. Press the seams open.

Bag Assembly

Body

1 Align piece C with the top of the appliqué Strip RST, and sew. Press the seam toward C, and topstitch the seam.

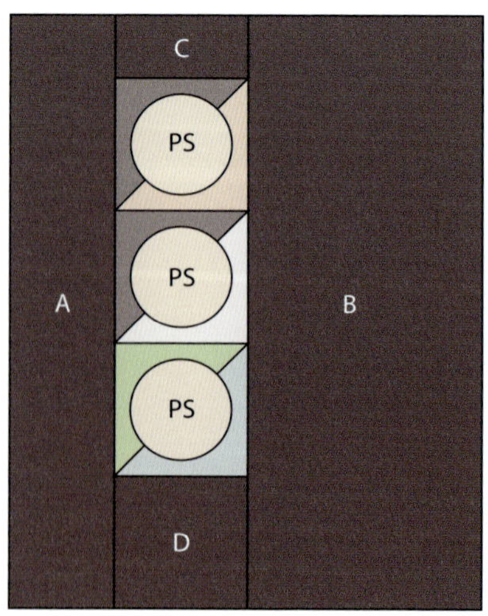

Finished bag exterior front diagram (PS represents the Patchwork Sashiko circles)

1

2. Align piece D with the bottom edge of the appliqué Strip RST, and sew. Press the seam toward D, and topstitch the seam. Trim piece D if the entire appliqué strip is longer than 18½″.
3. Sew piece A to the left edge of the appliqué Strip. Sew piece B to the right edge of the appliqué Strip. Press the seams away from the strip, and topstitch both seams. This is the finished Front Body.
4. Align the Front Body and piece E RST. Pin and sew together around the 2 sides and bottom, leaving the top open.

2

3a

3b

4

5 Fold the bag so the side seams are aligned in the center at the top edge. Pin at the folds to keep the seams centered. Align the side and bottom seams the same way, and pin or clip in place.

6 Measure 3″ across the corner with the 1½″ mark at the center seam. Draw a line, and sew over the line. Trim the corner ¼″ from the sewn line. Repeat on the other corner.

5a

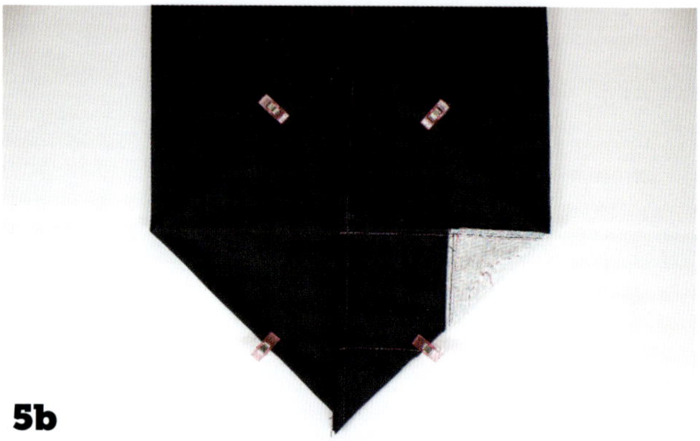

5b

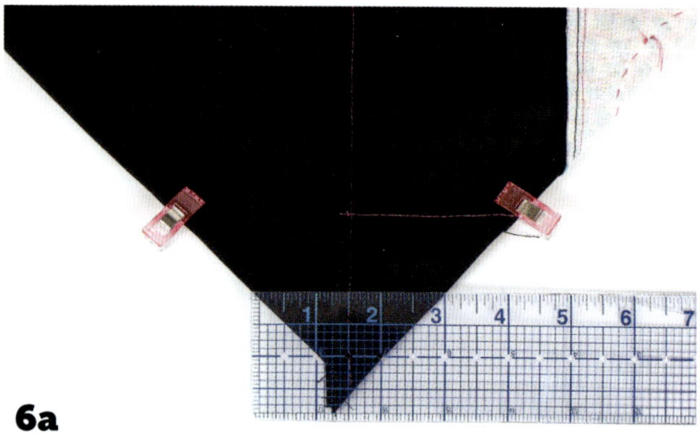

6a

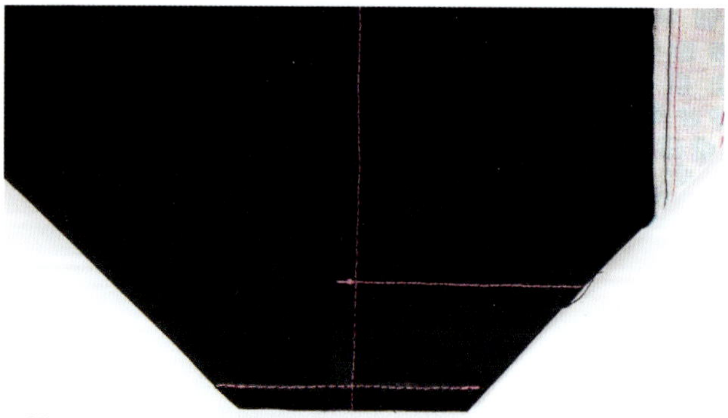

6b

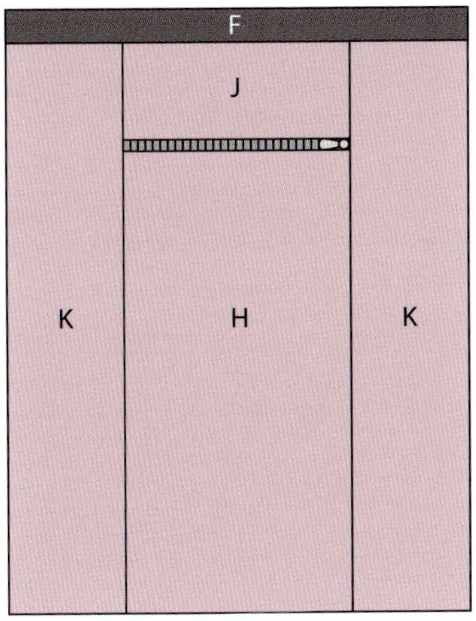

Lining pocket diagram

1

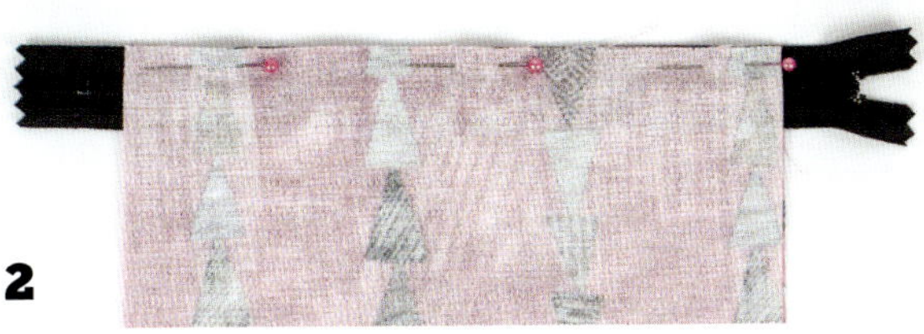

2

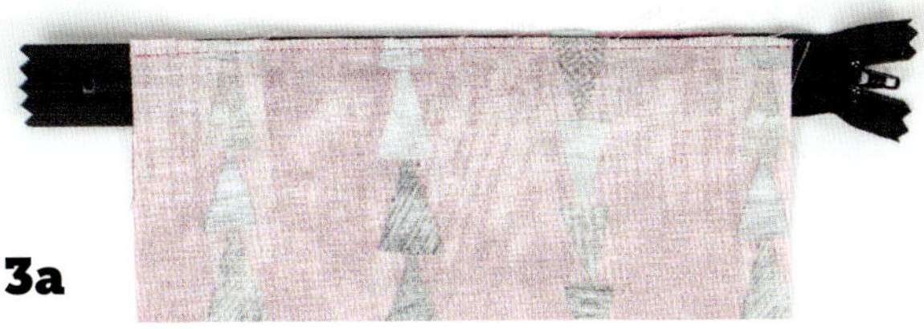

3a

Lining

When aligning the pieces for the zipper pocket, always have the 7½″ edges at the top and bottom.

1. Place piece G RS up. Position the zipper on top, RS up with the zipper pull to the right and the edge aligned to the top of G. Pin below the zipper teeth.
2. Place piece H on top of the zipper, RS down, and aligned with the top edge. Pin above the zipper teeth, and remove the pins from Step 1.
3. Sew along the top edge (see Keep in Mind!, page 47 for more on sewing zippers). Press pieces G and H away from the zipper. Topstitch.
4. Place piece I RS up. Align the zipper unit with the 7½″ edge (with piece H on top). Pin below the zipper teeth.

3b

4

5

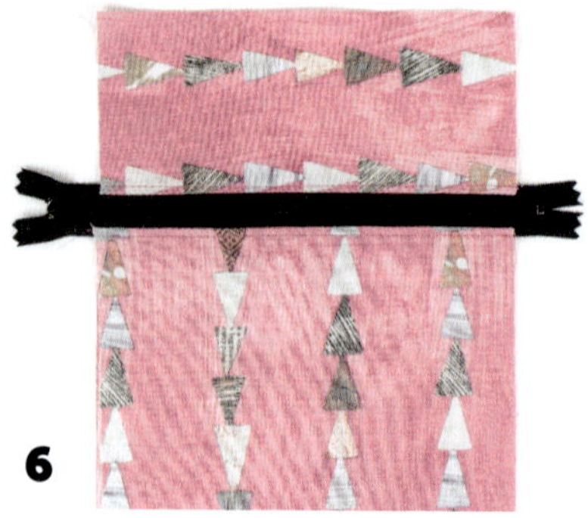

6

7

5 Align piece J on top, RS down. Pin above the zipper teeth, and remove the pins from Step 4.

6 Sew along the top edge (see Keep in Mind!, page 47 for more on sewing zippers). Press only piece J away from the zipper. Topstitch.

7 Lift up piece H (the long piece below the zipper). Pieces G and I should be aligned at the bottom edge. Pin pieces G and I together, then sew the bottom edge. Trim the bottom of piece H so that the length of the whole unit is 18½″ (if needed).

8 Move the zipper pull to the center. Sew piece K to each side of the unit from Step 7, RST. Pin along the edges before sewing, especially before and after the zipper and the bottom edge of the pocket on each side. Trim the excess zipper, and press the seams toward the K pieces. Topstitch.

8a

8b

9a

9b

9 Align a piece F and the top edge of the lining, RST. Sew together. Press the seam toward piece F. Topstitch.

10 Repeat Step 9 with the second piece F and the 14½″ edge of piece L.

11 Place the units from Step 9 and 10 RST, matching F strips. Sew together along the sides and bottom edges, leaving a 5″ gap in the center of the bottom seam. Don't sew along the top edge.

12 Repeat Steps 5–6 in Body (page 56) to make boxed corners in the lining.

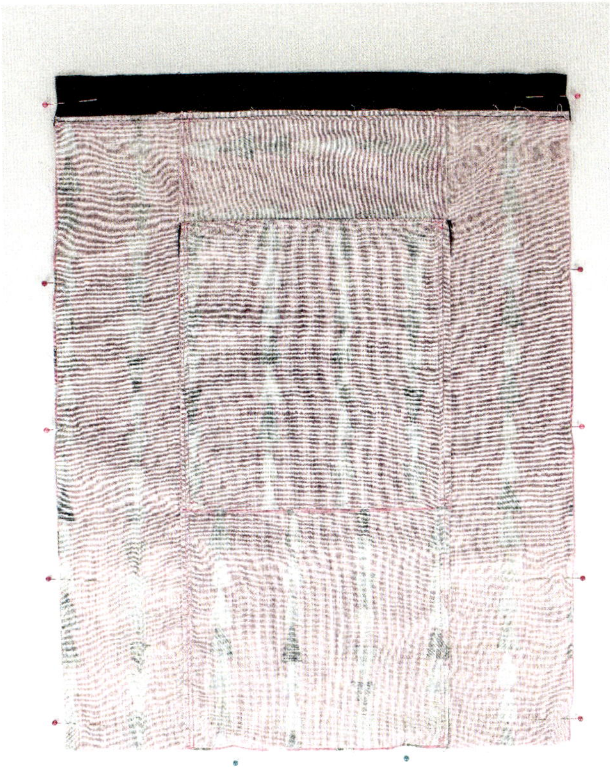

11

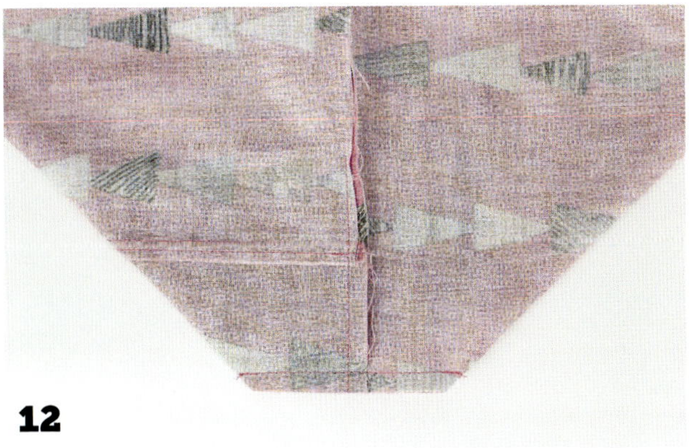

12

1a

1b

Handles

1 Fold each handle piece lengthwise WST, and press. Fold each long edge to the center crease WST, and press. Refold the strap in half, enclosing the raw edges. Topstitch along both folds.

NOTE • *Fabric pictured for the strap creation and attachment is a different color for visibility.*

2 On the RS of the exterior front, make a mark 3¾″ inward from both side seams along the top edge. Repeat on the exterior back.

3 Center the ends of one handle with the marks on the front 1″ past the raw edge of the bag. Pin. Baste to the bag with a long straight stitch as close as possible to the edge of the bag. Repeat on the back with the other strap.

// Watch the Handle Twist! // *When basting the handle to the body, make sure the handles aren't twisted.*

1c

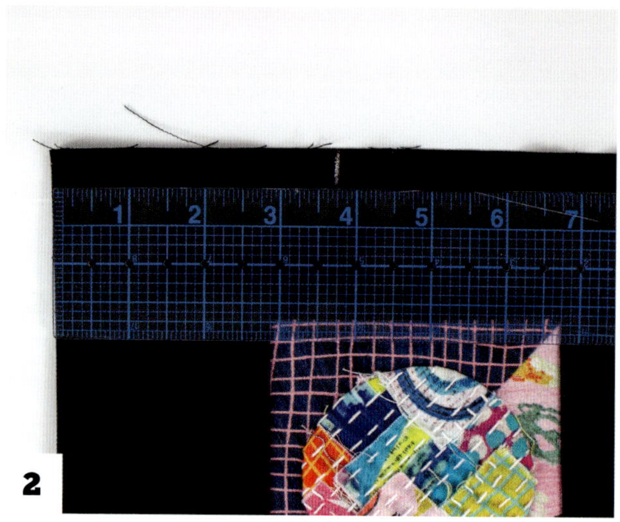

2

3

1

2

Final Assembly

1 With the exterior RS out and the lining WS out, stuff the body into the lining. The zipper pocket should be aligned with the back exterior. Match the side seams, then adjust, aligning the raw top edges. Pin together.

// No Crooked Handles! // *Even though the handles are basted in place, they can become skewed when you sew the top edges together. Insert a pin perpendicular to the top edge to prevent the handles from shifting.*

2 Sew all the way around the top of the bag. Pull the exterior through the opening in the bottom of the lining.

3 Tuck the raw edges of the lining gap to the WS, and press. Pin closed, then sew with a topstitch.

4 Push the lining into the bag. Press the top of the bag. Topstitch around the top, then again ⅞″ below the top. Add extra stitching (in an X shape) where the handles are attached to the bag.

3a

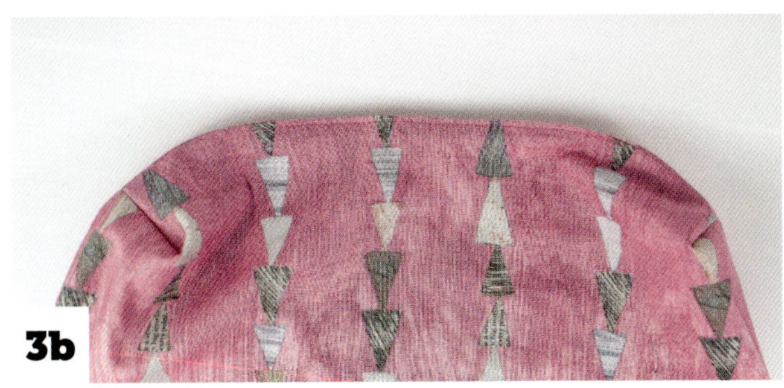

3b

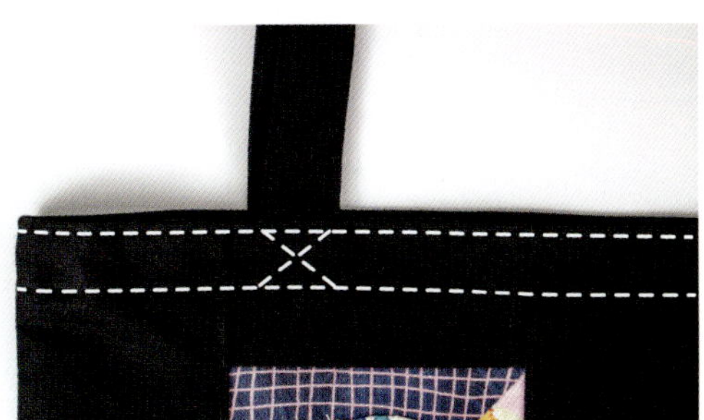

4

Triple Moon Zipper Bag

FINISHED SIZE: Approximately 9″ × 4″ × 3″

This bag features an accent panel and three appliqué circles that hang like moons from ribbons. Instead of using scrappy Patchwork Sashiko textiles, the moons are made from a single layer of fabric that is stitched for texture. But, if you prefer, you can choose to use a finished Patchwork Sashiko textile for the moons. Bright and cheery fabrics bring out a modern abstract style while subdued fabrics can bring out a poignant and quiet mood.

MATERIALS

- Fat quarter of quilting cotton or linen fabric (for exterior)
- Fat quarter of quilting cotton (for bag lining and accent panel)
- Scraps of quilting cotton in 3 prints or colors (for the appliqué)
- 1¼ yards of ⅜″-wide ribbon
- 12″ zipper, size #3 or #5
- ¼ yard of Pellon P44F Fusible Interfacing
- ¼ yard of Bosal In-R-Form Single Sided Fusible Foam Stabilizer
- ⅛ yard of Pellon 70 Peltex
- Crewel needle, size 2
- Cotton crochet thread, size 10 in white
- Triple Moon Templates 1 and 2

CUTTING LIST

Access the required templates by going to Templates (page 46). Template 1 is a 3″ diameter circle, and Template 2 is a 2″ diameter circle.

For the appliqué:

Cut 1 Triple Moon Template 1 from Peltex.

Cut 1 Triple Moon Template 2 from Peltex.

Cut 1 square 4″ × 4″ from each of 3 quilting cotton scraps.

Bag Exterior

For the bag exterior:

A: Cut 2 rectangles 6″ × 10″ from the bag exterior fabric

B: Cut 4 squares 1½″ × 1½″ from the bag exterior fabric

C: Cut 6 pieces 6½″ long from the ribbon

D: Cut 1 rectangle 2¼″ × 8″ from the lining/accent fabric

E: Cut 2 rectangles 6″ × 10″ from the Bosal foam

F: Cut 3 squares 4″ × 4″ from the P44F

G: Cut 1 rectangle 2¼″ × 8″ from the P44F

Bag Lining

H: Cut 2 rectangles 6″ × 10″ from the lining/accent fabric

Prepare the Materials

Fuse the E pieces to the WS of each A piece. Fuse the G piece to the WS of the D piece.

Appliqué Circles

1. Lay out the 4″ × 4″ quilting cotton squares. Draw a stitch line through the center of 1 square. Then, draw lines on either side, ¼″ apart. Draw 11 total lines per square. Repeat with the other 2 squares.

2. Start stitching on the lines using the same technique from the Patchwork Sashiko Method (see Hand Stitching, page 28). Begin with the middle line, then move outward. Repeat on all 3 squares.

IT'S A BREEZE! • *It's far easier to stitch through one layer of fabric! I encourage you to try and stitch each row in one pass, fitting all the folds from one line on the needle. Your stitches will be straighter, and this step will be finished in no time!*

3. Fuse the F pieces to the WS of the stitched squares.

1a

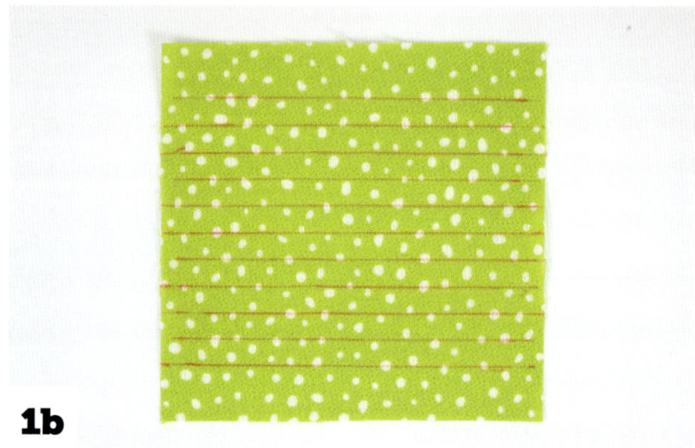

1b

2

3

4a

4b

4 Center Triple Moon Template 1 on the WS of each square (middle stitch line in the center). Trace and cut out the circles.

5 Cut a 36″ length of sewing thread and thread the crewel needle. Pull the thread through so it's doubled (18″ in length), and knot the ends together. Sew a running stitch around the perimeter of the circle, ¼″ from the edge and with a ¼″ stitch length. A longer stitch will result in a circle with a less smooth curve. Sew on the WS of the circle, and start with the needle going RS to WS (knot is on the RS). End the last stitch on the RS of the circle. Repeat on the other 2 circles.

6 Place the Template 2 Peltex in the center of the WS of a stitched circle. Gently pull on the needle, tightening the running stitch and curving the edges of the circle around the Peltex tightly. Tie a knot. Press the appliqué circle with the Peltex still inside, first with steam, then without steam. Remove the Peltex from the appliqué circle, and press again. Repeat Steps 5–6 for the other 2 circles.

5

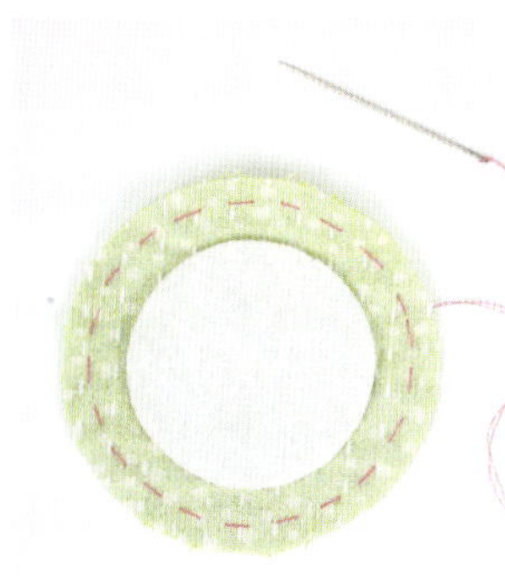

6a

6b

6c

1

2

Bag Assembly

1 Place 1 piece A horizontally on the work surface, RS up. Align D on top, RS up and centered along the top edge. Pin, and topstitch around all four raw edges of D.

2 Mark the top center of D. Then, mark 2¼″ on each side of the center. Repeat on the bottom edge. Draw 3 lines between the 3 marks.

3 Align 3 C ribbon pieces on the lines, making sure the ends extend just past the edges. Pin. Topstitch down the center of each ribbon.

// Glue it! // *Pinning ⅜″-wide ribbon can be tricky. Use fabric glue to adhere the ribbon to the fabric before sewing if you prefer.*

4 Repeat Steps 2–3 on the second A piece (omitting the D piece).

5 Align the center of the appliqué circles on the front A piece where the ribbons intersect the accent panel, and pin. The stitching should be vertical with the center line of stitching aligned with the ribbons.

3

4

5

6 Hand stitch the circles to the A piece using the crewel needle and crochet thread and a whipstitch (see Additional Stitching, page 36). Stitch around the edge of each circle. I like to divide the circle into quarters and place an even number of stitches in each section.

6

1a

1b

Zipper

1 Draw 2 lines on the RS of the zipper that are 8″ apart and equidistant from the center. Align the B squares with these lines on the side closest to the center, RS facing the zipper. Flip over, and pin 2 more B squares, sandwiching the zipper. Move the zipper pull to the center.

2 Sew a ¼″ seam perpendicular to the zipper along the outer edge of each B pair. Go slowly, being careful as you stitch over the zipper teeth. Press the B pieces away from the center of the zipper on both ends of the zipper. Topstitch.

3 Fold the B pieces to the center, and trim the excess zipper so there is only ¼″ remaining past each seam.

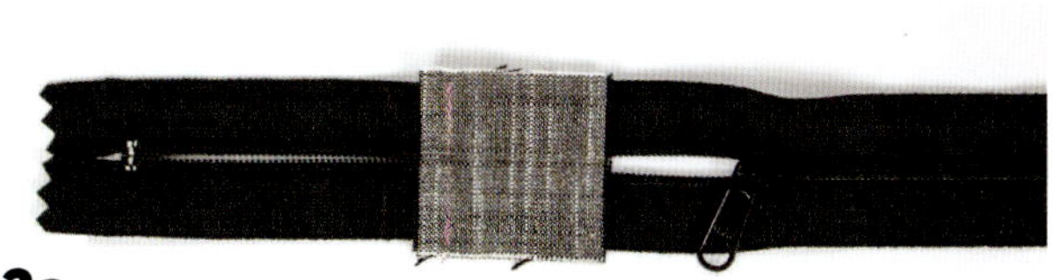

2a

2b

3a

3b

1

2

Final Assembly

1 Place the appliquéd exterior piece with the accent panel at the top, RS up. Center the zipper with the top edge, RS down. Align the zipper edge, not the B pieces. Make sure the zipper pull is to the left. Pin below the teeth.

2 Place 1 H piece RS down on top of the Step 1 unit. Pin above the zipper teeth, and remove the pins from Step 1. Sew along the top edge (see Keep in Mind!, page 47 for more on sewing zippers).

3 Press the body and lining WST, away from the zipper. Topstitch.

4 Align the Step 3 unit with the remaining exterior piece (the back), RST. Pin below the zipper teeth.

5 Place the second H piece RS down on top of the zipper (and RS of other H piece). Pin above the zipper teeth, and remove the pins from Step 4. Sew along the top edge (see Keep in Mind!, page 47 for more on sewing zippers).

3

4

5

6

7

8a

8b

8c

6 Press the body and lining, WST, away from the zipper. Topstitch.

7 Fold the unit so the exterior pieces are RST and the lining pieces are RST. Pin the bottom edges of the two pairs. On the exterior pieces, pay special attention to ensure the ribbons are aligned.

8 Unzip the zipper. Adjust the unit so that the B zipper ends are folded toward the lining. The seam allowances of both the exterior and lining pieces should point in the direction of the exterior fabric. Finally, make sure the topstitched edges of the exterior fabrics are matching. Pin on both sides of the zipper to keep the seams in place. Align the side edges, and pin.

9

10

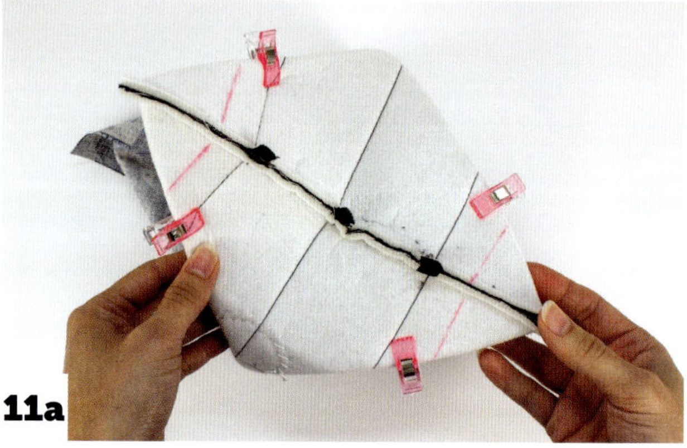

11a

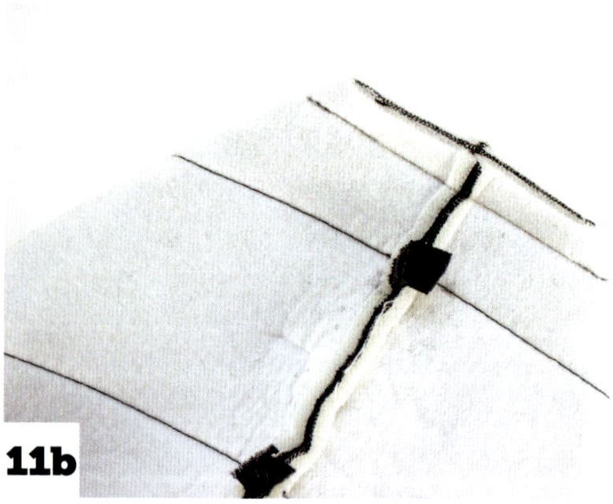

11b

12

9 Sew around the entire piece, leaving a 4″ gap in the center bottom edge of the lining.

10 Fold the corners of the bag so the bottom and side seams are aligned, and pin or clip in place.

11 Measure 3″ across the corner with the 1½″ mark at the center seam. Draw a line, and sew over the line. Trim the corner ¼″ from the sewn line. Repeat on the other exterior fabric corner as well as for both corners of the lining.

12 Reach into the gap in the lining and pull the exterior fabric through the lining. Use your fingers to push out the corners.

13 Tuck the raw edges of the lining gap to the WS, and press. Pin closed, then sew with a topstitch. Stuff the lining back into the bag.

14 Finger press the edges of the bag to highlight the structure and definition. Then, use an iron to carefully set the shape of the bag.

13

Pyramid Pouch

FINISHED SIZE: 4″ × 4″ × 4″

This project adds a little 3D interest to a traditional coin purse. The shape is reminiscent of the sticky rice and beans wrapped in banana leaves my mom would share with me and my brother in Taiwan!

MATERIALS

- 5″ × 9½″ interfaced Patchwork Sashiko Textile with stitching parallel to long edges (for pouch exterior)
- Fat eighth of quilting cotton (for lining)
- ¼ yard of Pellon 987F fusible fleece
- 7″ zipper, size #3
- 1½″ long piece of ½″-wide twill tape
- Swivel clasp, size ½″
- Keyring, size 1″
- Pencil, chopstick, or similar point turner

Notes on Patchwork Sashiko Textile

Start with a muslin base of 7″ × 11½″ to make a textile with a usable area of 5″ × 9½″ (after trimming). The stitching should be parallel to the long edge.

CUTTING LIST

Cut 1 rectangle 5″ × 9½″ from the lining fabric

Cut 1 rectangle 5″ × 9½″ from fusible fleece

Prepare The Materials

Fuse the fusible fleece 5″ × 9½″ rectangle to the WS of the 5″ × 9½″ Patchwork Sashiko rectangle.

Bag Assembly

1. Place the 5″ × 9½″ lining rectangle RS up with a short side at the top. Align the closed zipper to the top edge, RS up with the zipper pull to the left. Center so that 1″ of the zipper extends past the lining on both sides. Pin below the teeth.

2. Place the Patchwork Sashiko rectangle (bag exterior) RST on top of the zipper and lining, aligning the edges. Pin above the zipper teeth, but leave the end near the zipper pull unpinned.

1

2

3a

3b

3 Flip the unit over, and unzip the zipper halfway. Fold back the upper layer (zipper pinned to lining). Baste ½″–¾″ where the zipper and bag exterior edges meet at the corner. Fold the zipper end (past the basting) at a right angle away from the fabric. Clip in place, then baste over it (use a stiletto to hold the zipper while sewing if necessary).

4 Re-cover the zipper with the bag exterior, and pin over the zipper fold. Remove the pins from the lining.

5 Sew together along the top edge (see Keep in Mind!, page 47 for more on sewing zippers). Press the seams away from the zipper. Topstitch.

// The Zipper Pull // *Any time you are sewing a zipper and the zipper pull is impeding the presser foot, don't push through! Put the needle down through the layers, lift the presser foot, and then move the zipper pull away from the direction you're sewing.*

4

5a

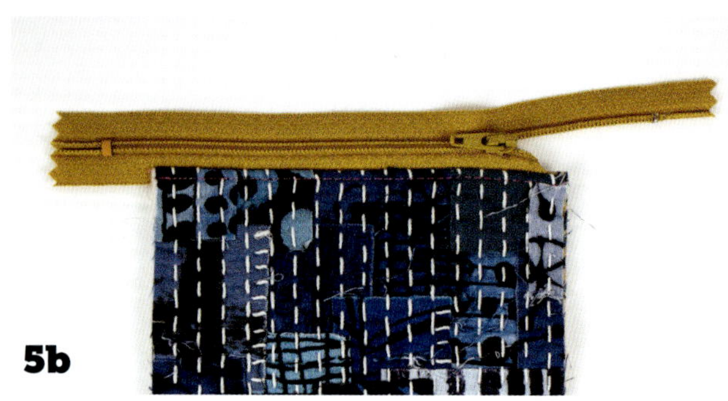
5b

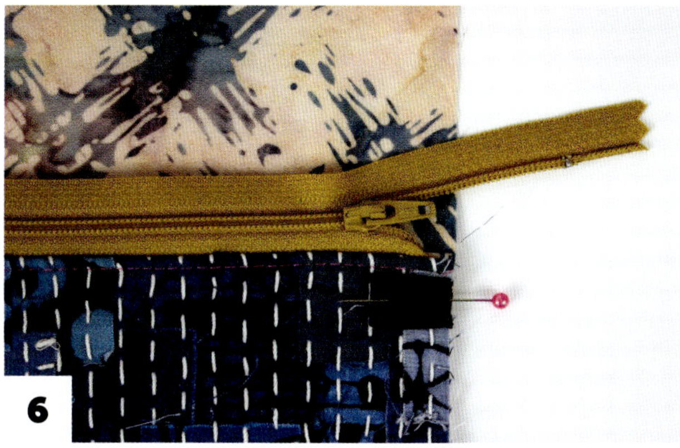
6

7

6 With the zipper closed, fold the lining out of the way. Fold the twill tape in half (short ends together). Align the twill tape on the RS of the bag exterior. The short raw ends should match up with the edge of the bag exterior, and the top edge should align with topstitching. Baste.

7 Flip the unit over so the lining is on top. Fold the bottom edge of the lining up to the top zipper edge (RST). Insert 2 pins below the zipper teeth, leaving the area near the zipper pull unpinned.

8 Flip the unit over. Fold the bottom edge of the bag exterior to match the top zipper edge, and insert 2 pins above the zipper teeth, leaving the area near the zipper pull unpinned.

9 Flip the unit back over, and fold back the lining. Baste ½″–¾″ where the zipper and bag exterior edges meet at the corner. Fold the zipper tail (past the basting) at a right angle away from the fabric. Clip in place, then baste over it (use a stiletto to hold the zipper while sewing if necessary).

10 Fold the lining back down. Flip the unit back over, and add another pin to the exterior. Remove the pins from the lining.

8

9a

9b

10

11a

11b

11 Sew together along the top edge (see Keep in Mind!, page 47 for more on sewing zippers). Press the seams away from the zipper. Topstitch.

12 Zip up the zipper and turn WS out.

13 Position the zipper in the center and flatten the lining on the bottom. Then, flatten the bag exterior on top. Pin all layers together near the end of the zipper.

12

13a

// Centering the Zipper // *Position the zipper at the center visually. Then, use a ruler to measure the distance from the zipper teeth to the outer folds. If the right and left fold measurements don't match, adjust the zipper position until they do.*

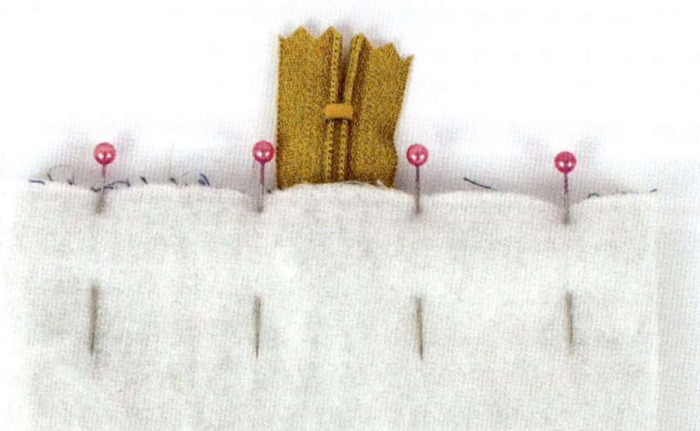

13b

14

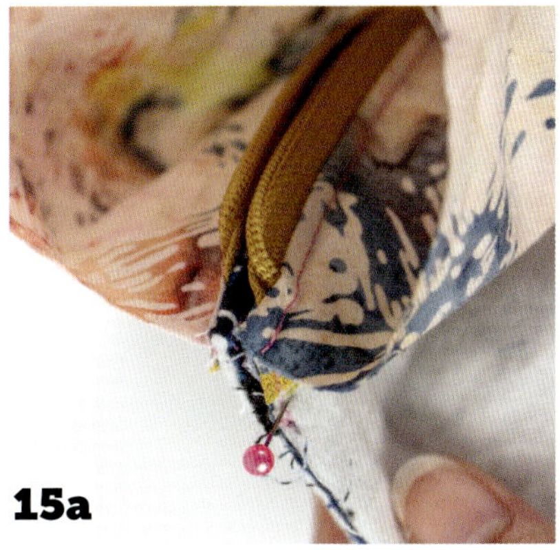

15a

15b

14 Sew together. Trim away the zipper excess with scissors.

15 Unzip the zipper. Fold the unsewn edges to meet on either side of the zipper (on the side where the zipper is folded) lining up the topstitching. Make sure the zipper teeth are pointed towards the lining and the zipper tape is towards the bag exterior. Pin near the zipper, then aligning the raw edges of both sides (lining to lining and exterior to exterior), pin all raw edges.

// Professional Bags // *The key to making sure your bag looks professional is to align the topstitching. If these are misaligned, it's very obvious when the pouch is turned right side out.*

16

17

18

19

16 Starting at the folded edge of the exterior fabric, sew 2″ past the zipper, leaving a gap in the lining. Carefully sew back and forth across the zipper a few times.

17 Turn the piece RS out through the gap in the lining, but keep the gap in the lining sticking out of the top. Use the pencil or similar tool to push out the corners of the pouch.

18 Tuck the raw edges of the lining gap to the WS, and press. Pin closed, then sew with a topstitch. Stuff the lining into the pouch.

19 Slide the swivel clasp onto the keyring, then attach the key ring to the twill loop.

4th Dimension Dumpling Pouch

FINISHED SIZE: 5″ × 3″ × 3″

Are you ready to enter the 4th dimension ...of scraps? This project takes Patchwork Sashiko textile scraps and single layer sashiko scraps (like those from the Triple Moon Zipper Bag, page 62) one step further.

MATERIALS

- 7″ × 9″ interfaced Patchwork Sashiko textile
- Fat eighth of quilting cotton or linen fabric (for pouch exterior)
- Fat eighth of quilting cotton (for lining and binding)
- ¼ yard of Bosal In-R-Form Single Sided Fusible Foam Stabilizer or Fusible Fleece Interfacing
- 14″ zipper, size #5
- Dumpling Template 1

Material Notes

I am using a metallic nylon zipper from a roll of zipper tape. It's a great option to get the look of metal but the ease of sewing with a nylon zipper. If you're using zipper tape by the yard, cut it to 14″ long and attach one zipper pull. Then, sew a few lines of stitching at the end to keep the pull from slipping off.

The instructions give you a choice of foam or fleece fusible interfacing. Foam will add more structure and make the quilting look more pronounced. Fleece will be softer and easier to manipulate as you're sewing.

Feel free to use Patchwork Sashiko scraps instead of a complete rectangle.

CUTTING LIST

Access the required templates by going to Templates (page 46).

Exterior

From the pouch exterior fabric:

A: Cut 1 rectangle 8″ × 11″ (for bag exterior)

B: Cut 2 rectangles 1¾″ × 2½″ (for exterior tabs)

Lining

From the lining fabric:

C: Cut 1 rectangle 8″ × 11″ (for bag lining)

D: Cut 2 rectangles 2½″ × 4″ (for gussets)

E: Cut 2 rectangles 1½″ × 3½″ (for binding)

F: Cut 1 fusible foam or fleece rectangle 8″ × 11″

Prepare The Materials

Fuse piece F to the WS of piece A.

Bag Assembly

Bag Body

1 Trace the outline of Dumpling Template 1 onto the upper half of the RS of the A rectangle. Flip the template over and trace the mirror image, connecting the two templates on the flat side.

1

2a

2b

2 Cut the Patchwork Sashiko textile into triangles that are about 2″ or smaller.

3 Staying within the boundaries of the traced template on A, lay out the triangle pieces. Try to keep the edges parallel to one another with about ¼″–⅜″ between them. There won't be perfect spacing but that's ok! Create a pattern that is visually pleasing to you. Pin.

PLACEMENT • *It's ok if some of the pieces extend past the template lines. In addition to this, the ¼″ seam allowance around the piece may intersect some triangles.*

4 Draw a line down the center of the Step 3 unit. Sew on the line, overlapping the triangles as necessary. Use a stiletto and go very slow over the triangles.

// Thread Color // *When I quilt a project, I typically choose a thread that is lighter in color than the majority of the body fabric. In this case, a lighter thread will show the individual quilting stitches more clearly amid a variety of background fabrics.*

3

4

5

6

5 Measure and mark lines each ⅜″ apart to the right and left of the center line. Sew on top of the lines, repeating Step 4. You don't have to sew all the way to the edges of the rectangle—just quilt at least ½″ beyond the traced template lines.

LOOSE EDGES • *Some of the edges of the triangle scraps will be loose. That's okay! Because the scraps have P44F interfacing fused to the back, the hand stitching will not unravel and will be stable, even as the edges fray over time.*

6 Place the template on top of piece A again. If it no longer matches up, retrace the template. Cut out the bag exterior on the template lines (do not cut through the middle line).

7 Repeat Step 1 with the C rectangle. Cut the lining out.

Tabs

1 Fold each B piece in half, RST and matching short ends. Sew the raw edges together.

2 Turn the tabs RS out and press so that the seam is centered. Topstitch the folded edges. Fold in half again, short sides together, and press.

1

2a

2b

3a

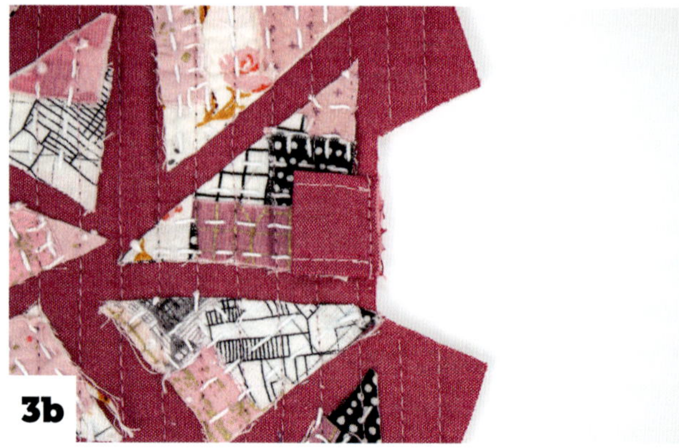
3b

3 Center the tabs on the indented edges of the bag exterior, aligning the raw edges and pin. Baste in place.

Gussets

Fold each D piece in half, WST and matching short edges. Press. Topstitch the fold, and baste the raw edges.

Final Assembly

1 Draw a line on the WS of the zipper 2½″ from the end. Make small cuts no deeper than ¼″ about 1″ apart down the entire length of the zipper on both edges.

2 Open the zipper. Align the line on the zipper, RST, to the corner of the bag exterior at the end of one curve as shown. Pin the zipper around the curve, and then slowly baste. Repeat on the other curve with the other side of the zipper.

1

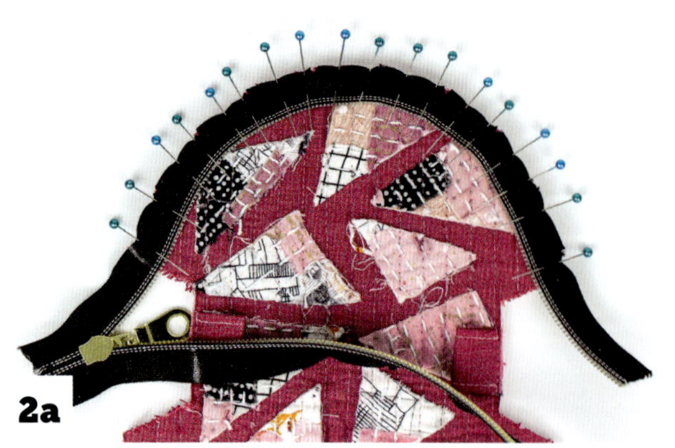
2a

2b

3a

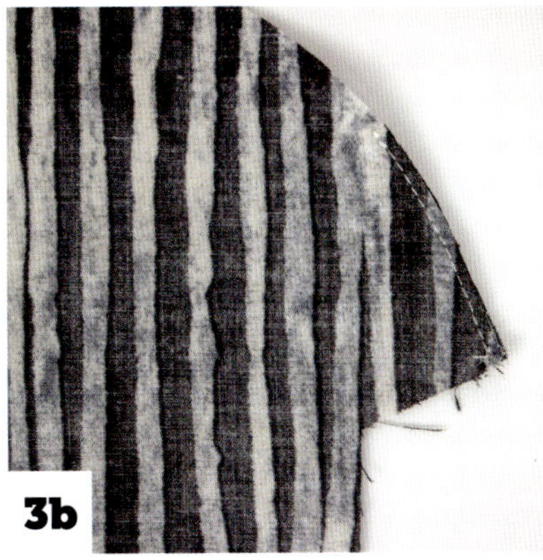

3b

4

3 Pin and baste the gussets onto the RS of piece C as shown. Don't try to line up the straight edge to the curve. Sew from the WS of the lining and follow the curve, then trim the excess gusset.

4 Pin the opposite side of the gussets to the other side of the curve (piece C should be WS out), and repeat Step 3 to attach the gussets to the other side.

5 With the Step 4 unit WS out, align one curved edge, RST, with one curved edge of the bag exterior and zipper. Pin around the curve, then sew (see Keep in Mind!, page 47 for more on sewing zippers). Repeat on the other side of the lining, bag exterior, and zipper, folding it into position to align the second curve.

// Don't Stretch the Lining // *Sometimes, you might accidentally stretch a piece of fabric while pinning around a curve. To avoid this, place a couple pins at the beginning and end before placing all the pins in between.*

5a

5b

5c

6

7a

6 Turn the pouch RS out and press the curved edges. Topstitch the curves.

7 Zip up the pouch about 4″ and turn so the lining is facing out. Push the zipper ends through the openings on each side by the gussets, but keep the tabs inside of the pouch. Fold the ends of the pouch so the edges are aligned. Make sure the tabs are centered over the zipper. Pin, and sew the edges closed. Trim the excess zipper on both ends to ¼″.

8 Center and align a long raw edge of binding piece E to a raw edge from Step 7, RST. Pin, then sew from the side opposite the binding, matching up with the seams from Step 7.

9 Fold the binding piece away from the seam, and press.

7b

8

9

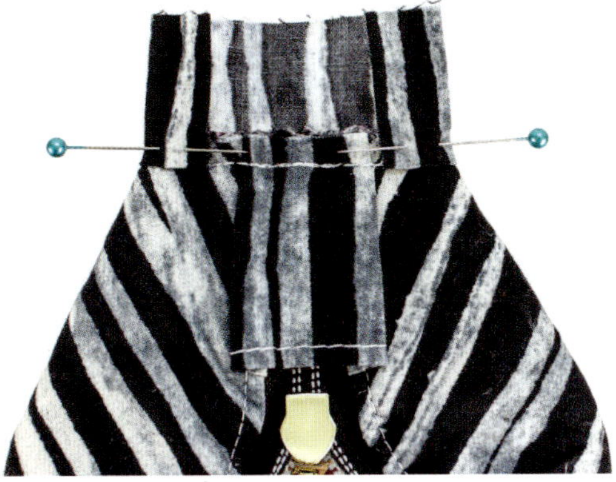

10a

10b

10 Fold the short ends of the binding toward the center, WST. Pin. Then, fold the top edge of the binding ¼″ to the WS, press, and then another ¼″ so the fold covers the seam from Step 8. Pin, then topstitch, holding the seam with a stiletto.

11 Repeat Steps 8–10 on the other side. Turn the bag right side out.

11

Upcycled Pincushion

FINISHED SIZE: 4″ × 4″

Confession. I have a weak spot for pincushions. Choose polyester fill, walnut shells, or a combination of both. Walnut shells make the pincushion heavier and stay in place better while using than with polyester fill alone. It's also said that the shells have a sharpening effect on your needles.

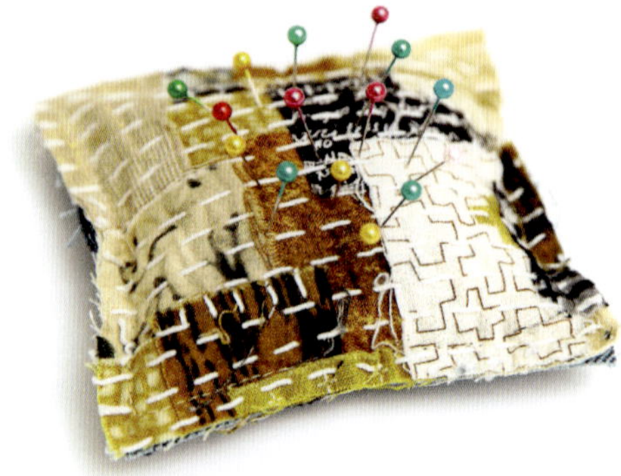

MATERIALS

- 4″ × 4″ interfaced Patchwork Sashiko textile
- 4″ × 4″ scrap of denim (or other heavyweight fabric)
- 1–2 cups of polyester fill and/or crushed walnut shells
- Crewel needle, size 2
- Cotton crochet thread, size 10 in white

Material Notes

Crushed walnut shells may also be labeled as "ground" walnut shells. They can be found specifically labeled as pincushion filling or it is commonly sold as reptile bedding. Choose a pair of jeans to upcycle that are 100% cotton and have no stretch. I also like to incorporate a jeans seam in my projects to add some extra interest.

Pincushion Assembly

1. Layer the Patchwork Sashiko piece and denim WST. Sew around the perimeter of the squares, leaving a 1″ gap in the center of 1 side. On the fourth side, sew just 1″ to leave a gap.
2. Carefully spoon walnut shells or stuff polyfill into the pincushion using scrap paper as a funnel if desired. Make sure you're filling it fully, tapping it down to fill all the corners and edges.
3. Pinch the gap closed, making sure there is still about ½″ of wiggle room unfilled. Pin, and sew the gap closed with a ¼″ seam, matching the line sewn in Step 1.

1

2

3

Come for Dinner, Stay for the Hot Pad

FINISHED SIZE: 8″ × 8″

I'm not much of a cook, but I do like to bake! This hot pad adds a useful bit of style to your kitchen with abstract patchwork and multi-colored hand stitching. It's a great way to use up scraps, and it makes a memorable gift.

MATERIALS

- Large scraps of quilting cotton in 4 different colors
- ⅛ yard of quilting cotton (for binding)
- 1 square 8″ × 8″ of quilting cotton (for back)
- 2 squares 8″ × 8″ of 100% cotton batting
- Crewel needle, size 2
- Cotton crochet thread, size 10 in 3 different colors
- Hot Pad Templates 1 and 2

CUTTING LIST

Access the required templates by going to Templates (page 46). Prepare the templates by printing them, and then cutting them out of the paper.

From Quilting Cotton 1:

A: Cut 1 rectangle 1½″ × 1¾″

B: Cut 1 rectangle 1½″ × 3½″

C: Cut 1 rectangle 2¼″ × 4¾″

D: Cut 1 rectangle 3¼″ × 3¾″

From Quilting Cotton 2:

E: Cut 1 Template 1

F: Cut 1 rectangle 1½″ × 8″

From Quilting Cotton 3:

G: Cut 1 Template 2

From Quilting Cotton 4:

H: Cut 1 rectangle 1¼″ × 3½″

From binding fabric:

Cut 1 strip 2¼″ × 36″

Pieced Top

While this pieced top shows off many of the beautiful elements of Patchwork Sashiko textiles, you can use an actual Patchwork Sashiko textile for this top if you prefer. Use a piece 8″ × 8″.

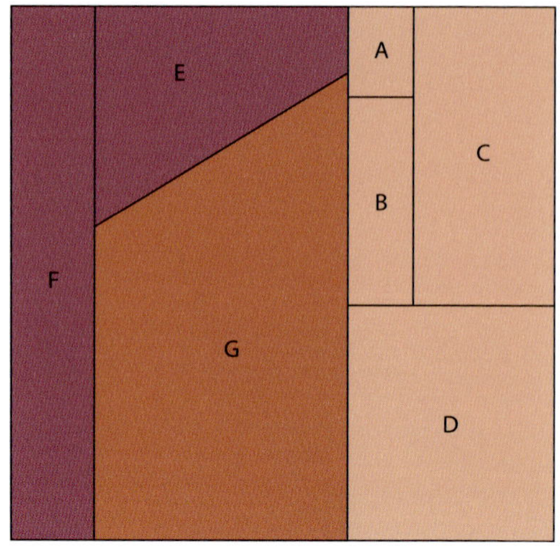

Piecing diagram

1. Sew together pieces A and B along the 1½″ edge, RST. Press the seam toward piece A.
2. Sew the Step 1 unit to the 4¾″ edge of piece C. Press the seam toward piece C.

// Which Way Should I Press? // *Potato, potahto, tomato, tomahto. Everyone has a personal preference when it comes to pressing seams. If one side of a seam has darker fabric than the other, I tend to press toward that side. If I'm not worried about darker fabric, I press toward the side that I think looks visually better from the RS.*

3. Sew the Step 2 unit to the 3¼″ edge of piece D to complete Section 1. Press the seam toward piece D.

1 **2** **3**

4a

4b

5

4 Place pieces E and G RST, diagonal edges aligned. Shift the pieces so the tips extend by ¼″. Sew together, and press the seam toward piece E. This is Section 2.

5 Sew Section 2 and piece F together along the 8″ edge. Press the seam toward Piece F.

6 Sew the Step 5 unit and Section 1 together along the 8″ edge as shown. Press the seam toward Section 1, then press the whole top.

6

Sashiko Stitching

Use the Patchwork Sashiko method to hand stitch the drawn lines (see Hand Stitching, page 28), but don't leave loops between lines of stitching.

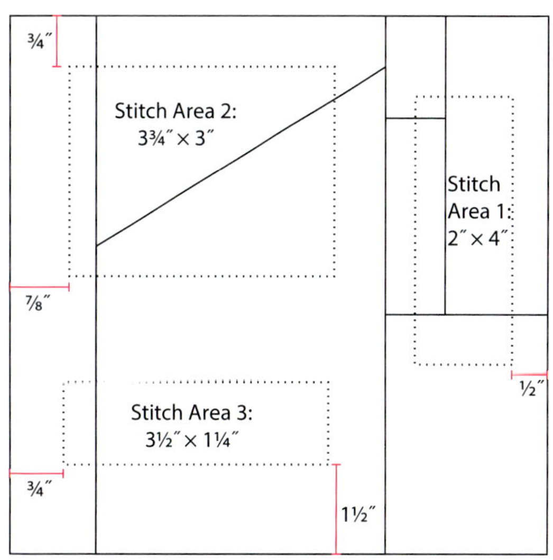

Stitching Diagram

1

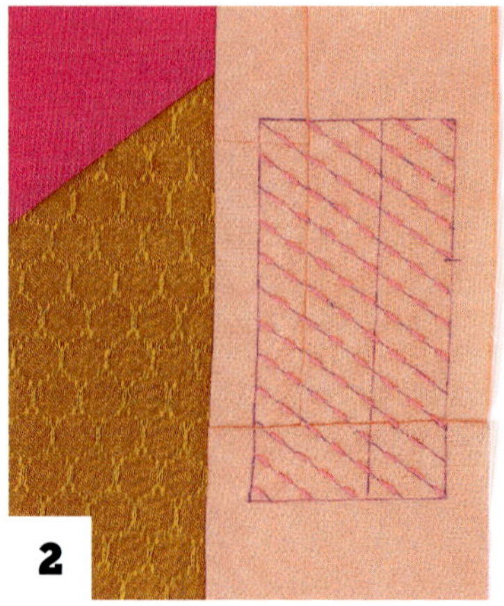
2

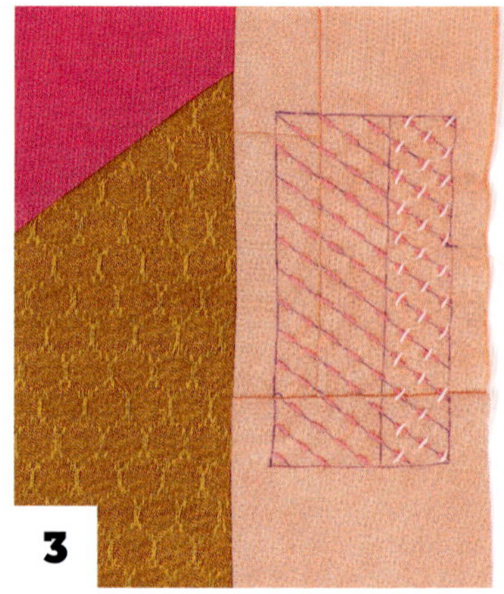
3

1. Use the Stitching Diagram to mark the rectangle for Stitch Area 1. Mark 1½″ down from the upper right corner of the rectangle, then draw a diagonal line from the mark to the upper left corner. Use this line as a guide and draw diagonal lines ¼″ apart across the entire rectangle. Draw a vertical line ¾″ from the right edge of the rectangle.
2. Hand stitch a running stitch on the diagonal lines with one color of crochet thread.
3. With a different color of thread, use single stitches to create an *X* on top of the running stitches to the right of the vertical line. Lift up the fabric while adding these stitches.
4. Use the stitching placement diagram to mark the Stitch Area 2 rectangle. Draw vertical lines ¼″ apart across the rectangle.

4

5

6

7

5. Hand stitch a running stitch on the lines with the same crochet thread used in Step 3. Do not stitch the top or bottom border lines.
6. Using the same thread color, stitch over the running stitch to create plus signs for all the stitches that do not fall on the G piece.
7. Use the stitching placement diagram to place the piece H rectangle for Stitch Area 3. Pin in place.

8

9

8 Draw lines horizontally ¼″ apart across the piece, continuing to mark one line above and below the piece. Extend the lines ¼″–½″ beyond the edges.

9 Hand stitch a running stitch on the lines with the third crochet thread color.

10 Remove all drawn stitch lines.

Final Assembly

1 Place the 8″ × 8″ back fabric RS down, layer the 2 layers of batting on top, and then place the pieced top RS up on top. Trim ⅛″ from all four sides, through all layers.

2 Pin, then baste around all 4 edges.

3 Fold the binding strip in half, WST, matching long edges. Pin every 2″. Mark 4″ from one of the ends. Then, pin that mark to 1½″ away from a bottom corner on the back of the hot pad, aligning raw edges.

1

2

3

4a

4b

4c

4. Sew the binding to the hot pad, starting at the mark and going toward the closest corner. Stop sewing ¼″ from the corner. Fold the binding at a right angle to the seam, then fold it on itself so that the binding is following the next edge. Begin sewing again. Repeat at each corner. Sew past the fourth corner 1½″ and stop.
5. Overlap the 2 loose ends of binding with the longer piece on top. Mark the top piece where the bottom piece ends. Measure 2¼″ past the mark, then cut away the excess binding of the top piece.
6. Unfold and unpin the ends of the binding. Mark 2¼″ from the end of the binding on the right binding piece. Place the raw edges of the two ends at a right angle RST, folding the hot pad as necessary. Pin. Draw a diagonal line from corner to corner referencing the 2¼″ mark, then sew on the line.

5

6a

6b

7a

7b

8a

8b

7 Trim excess fabric past the seam, and finger press the seam to one side. Re-fold the binding, and then finish sewing the binding to the hot pad.

8 Fold the binding over the raw edge onto the RS of the hot pad, and clip or pin. Use a zig-zag stitch to sew the binding to the RS. Use a stiletto to help guide the binding fold. Fold mitered corners before sewing over them.

Cozy Up Scarf

FINISHED SIZE: 7½″ × 59″

Wouldn't it be glorious to wear a scarf made entirely from a Patchwork Sashiko textile? The standard method textiles are a little too thick to wear this way, and they use tiny pieces that would take a lot of time to hand stitch across such a large textile. Can we get around that? You bet! Double gauze fabric is light, airy and very pliable, making it perfect for this project.

MATERIALS

- ½ yard of 60″-wide double gauze fabric (for the base layer and back)
- ⅛ yard each of double gauze fabric in 5 colors (for the patchwork)
- Crewel needle, size 2
- Wonderfil Eleganza Perle Cotton, size 5 or 8

CUTTING LIST

A: Cut 2 rectangles 8″ × WOF from the base layer and back double gauze

B: Cut 5 squares 3¾″ × 3¾″ from each color of double gauze (25 total)

C: Cut 5 rectangles 3¾″ × 5⅝″ from each color of double gauze (25 total)

Cut additional pieces if needed.

Patchwork Sashiko

As I mentioned in Change It Up! (page 40), you can modify the classic Patchwork Sashiko method to suit different scales and materials. Refer to Patchwork Sashiko Method Basics (page 18) for a refresher.

1. Measure and draw a line across one A rectangle every 12″. This makes 5 sections that are each 8″ × 12″ for the Patchwork Sashiko method.
2. Place 2 pieces of the same color gauze diagonal from one other (the origin spots) using any combination of B and C pieces. Layer 2 pieces each of the rest of the colors, overlapping each piece by a minimum of ½″ to fill the section. Pieces from each section can and should extend beyond the lines.

1

2

3a

3b

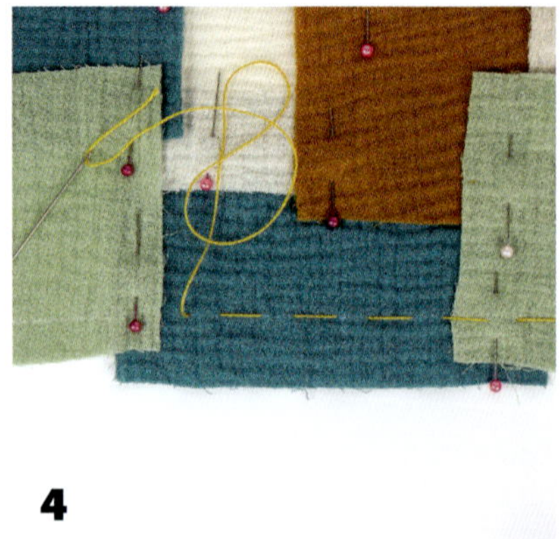

4

3 Insert straight pins parallel to the short edges of the base to keep the pieces in place. Repeat Steps 2–3 for each section.

4 Draw the first line for hand stitching ½″ away from and parallel to one long edge of the base. Hand stitch the line, but refer to the sidebar for changes in the stitching process.

5a

Stitching The Scarf

While hand stitching this project, follow these guidelines:

- Stitch length is ½″ long
- Spacing between hand-stitched lines is ½″
- Double gauze has a looser weave than quilting cotton, so move it carefully
- Knot at the end of every row (don't leave loops or continue stitching)
- Don't leave slack in the thread when knotting
- You likely don't need needle pullers, as the fabric is so light and thin

MESSY • *You've probably noticed by now that double-gauze will fray if it catches you staring at it. It's a good thing and a bad thing. It looks beautiful and ragged at the same time, and it's probably leaving thread everywhere. When you wash this scarf, place it into some kind of closed cotton or tightly woven mesh bag first.*

5b

5 Continue drawing lines and stitching across the entire scarf.

6 **Optional:** Apply some additional stitching to tack down loose edges (see Additional Stitching, page 36). It's unlikely that you will find any of the base fabric exposed in this project, but, take a look. If something bothers you, stitch it down!

5c

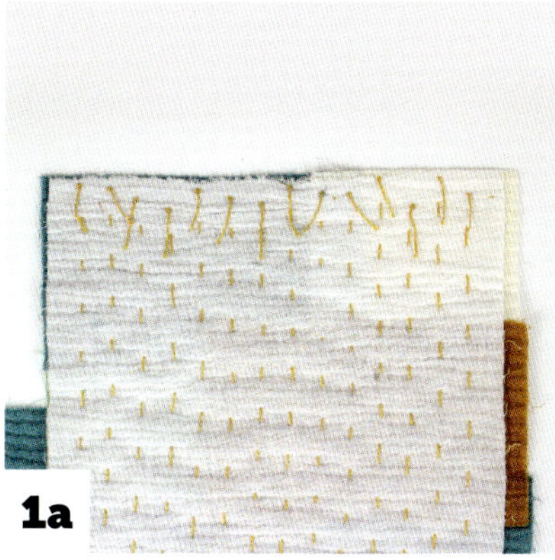

1a

1b

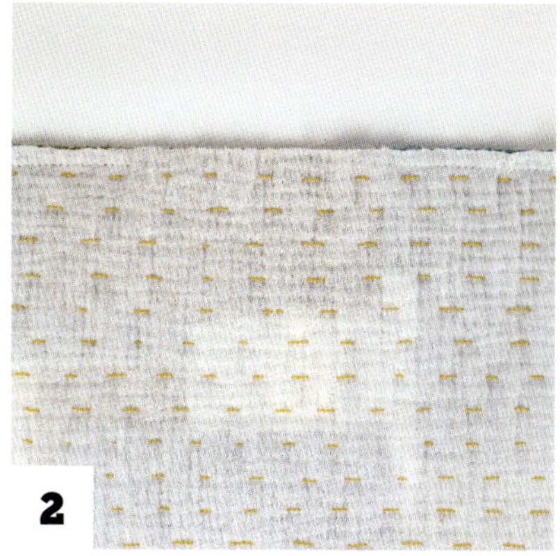

2

Finish the Scarf

// Exposed Stitching on the Back // *If you prefer to leave the stitching on the backside of the scarf visible, trim away all the patchwork pieces that extend past the base. Then, hem the edges to the back side with a ⅜″ double fold, tucking knot tails into the folds. Topstitch the hem.*

1. Press any knot tails at the edges of the scarf toward the center of the scarf on the back side. Lay the scarf WS up, and then trim away any patchwork pieces past the base. Do not cut through any stitch lines.
2. Lay the scarf and remaining piece A RST. Trim any excess and pin. Sew a ¼″ seam around all 4 sides, leaving a 4″ gap in one of the long edges.
3. Turn the scarf RS out, push out the corners, and press. Fold the gap in toward the WS, hiding the raw edges, and pin. Topstitch around all 4 edges.

3

Framed Patchwork Sashiko

FINISHED SIZE: 11″ × 14″

This project uses the same-sized textile you created in the Patchwork Sashiko basics section! If you haven't decided what to do with it yet, this might be perfect. Or, customize the size of the mat and backer board to make this work with any textile.

MATERIALS

- 7″ × 9″ Patchwork Sashiko textile
- 11″ × 14″ mat backing board
- 11″ × 14″ mat frame (inner opening 8½″ × 11″)
- Mini high temperature glue gun and glue sticks
- 11″ × 14″ frame
- 7″ × 9″ rectangle of Pellon P44F Interfacing (optional)

Mount

1. If needed, press the textile. If you prefer, fuse the P44F Interfacing to the back of the textile, and trim any excess interfacing.
2. Glue the mat frame to the backing board with a ⅜″ bead of glue onto each corner.
3. Center the textile inside the frame. Carefully lift a corner, then add a ⅜″ bead of glue onto the textile. Press textile to the mat backing board with your fingers. Repeat on each corner. If you like, sign and date the mat frame. Insert into the frame.

2

3

Main Event Embellished Top

I hope you like attention, because when you wear this garment, you'll be getting a lot of it! Choose a garment like a light denim shirt or a blazer that will contrast with the raw edged patchwork and hand stitching. Make sure the garment is made of woven (non-stretch) fabric. The top I chose is 100% cotton chambray (denim color) purchased from a thrift shop.

MATERIALS

- Woven top that opens in the front
- Scraps of quilting cotton in at least five different prints or colors
- Crewel needle, size 2
- Cotton crochet thread, size 10 in white
- Small flexible plastic cutting kitchen board (optional; single-use for this project)

CUTTING LIST

From each of the quilting cotton scraps, cut:

2–3 squares 1½″ × 1½″

2–3 rectangles 1½″ × 2¼″

This is a project that doesn't need to adhere as strictly to the standard Patchwork Sashiko method patchwork piece guidelines if you don't want it to. Feel free to cut all manner of shapes and sizes.

Balancing Embellishments

When adding just one area of patchwork, I suggest locating it towards the top or bottom of the garment, not centering it. If you add a few areas of patchwork around the garment, aim for a balanced look. I think of each side of the garment like a see-saw, with the center of the garment as the fulcrum. If you place embellishments in the top left, placing another area of embellishment in the bottom right will balance things out. Adding smaller patchwork areas to the back of the garment also helps to create a cohesive design. Repeat Steps 1–4 wherever you want to add a Patchwork Sashiko section.

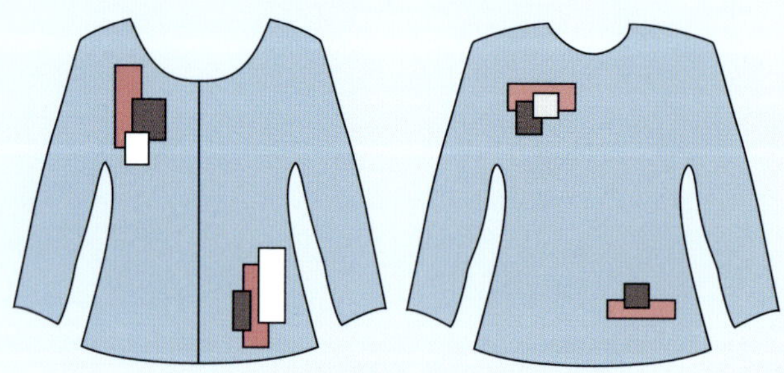

Balanced embellishments

1

2a

2b

3

Patchwork Sashiko

1 Cut the flexible cutting mat to the size of the area you are embellishing (in my case 6″ × 11″), or a little smaller. Use this board to ensure you're stitching only through the first layer of the garment. Lay it between the front and back of the garment, or within a pocket if applicable. You can also manipulate the garment to achieve one layer of fabric for hand stitching, but be careful to avoid warped stitch lines.

2 Using the Patchwork Sashiko method (see Laying the Patchwork, page 18), layer the quilting cotton pieces. Pin them with as few pins as possible, and skip basting stitches.

3 Draw the first stitch line on the right or left side of the design, overlapping the first patchwork piece. Hand stitch using the Patchwork Sashiko method (see Securing the Patchwork, page 26).

// New Rows // *The garment needs to be turned 180° each time you start a new row. However, if this becomes annoying, knot off your thread at the end of each row and start a new piece of thread. I also suggest doing this where there's a large distance between where one row ends and the next begins. Don't leave loops or slack in the thread.*

Piece of cutting board inserted into pocket before stitching

4a

4b

4c

4 Continue drawing lines ¼″ apart and stitching them one at a time until the entire area is covered and all the pieces are secured. Extend the stitch lines beyond the patchwork pieces by ½″–1″. Consider adding stitch lines that don't cross any patchwork pieces. As needed, lift up pieces like the pocket flaps to stitch beneath them.

NO INTERFACING NEEDED! • *No need to add interfacing to the finished patchwork. It will be stable and comfortable as is; wash it and wear it—it will be fine.*

Favorite Things Hexie Project Bag

FINISHED SIZE: 6″ × 10″ × 6″

I love drawstring bags! They are so versatile and more fun than a flat, zippered bag. This one is especially useful because it's designed for carrying your Patchwork Sashiko supplies with you.

MATERIALS

- 8″ × 11″ interfaced Patchwork Sashiko textile with stitching parallel to the short edges (for hexies)
- Large scraps of quilting cottons in 5 different prints or colors (for hexies)
- Fat eighth quilting cotton (for bag exterior and bottom)
- ⅝ yard quilting cotton (for lining and drawstring top)
- ½ yard of Pellon P44F lightweight interfacing
- ¼ yard Bosal In-R-Form Single Sided Fusible Foam
- ¾ yard of 1″-wide cotton or polyester webbing (for strap)
- 1¾ yards ⅜″-wide satin ribbon (for drawstring)
- Crewel needle, size 2
- Safety pin
- Cotton crochet thread, size 10 in white
- Standard 50-weight sewing machine thread
- Fabric glue or lighter (optional)
- Acrylic hexagon template for 1¼″ hexies with ⅜″ seam allowance (optional)
- Favorite Things Templates 1 and 2
- Favorite Things Hexagon Templates 1 and 2

CUTTING LIST

Access the templates in Templates (page 46). This book includes templates for a hexagon with 1¼″ length sides (one with ⅜″ seam allowance, and one without). You can use the provided templates, or purchase paper or acrylic templates. Prepare the templates by printing and then cutting them out of the paper. Prepare 1 copy of Favorite Things Hexagon Template 1 using cardstock. Prepare 21 copies of Favorite Things Hexagon Template 2 using cardstock.

From the scraps of quilting cotton:

Cut 1 rectangle 4″ × 12″ from each of 5 fabrics.

From the Pellon P44F Interfacing

Cut 5 rectangles 4″ × 12″.

From the bag exterior fabric:

A: Cut 1 rectangle 7″ × 12″

B: Cut 1 square 7½″ × 7½″

From the lining/drawstring top fabric:

C: Cut 2 rectangles 6½″ × 11″

D: Cut 2 rectangles 6″ × 11″

E: Cut 2 Favorite Things Template 1

F: Cut 4 rectangles 4½″ × 11″

G: Cut 2 strips 2″ × 10½″

From the Bosal Fusible Foam:

H: Cut 1 rectangle 7″ × 12″

I: Cut 1 rectangle 6½″ × 11″

J: Cut 1 square 7½″ × 7½″

From the ribbon:

Cut 2 pieces 30″ long.

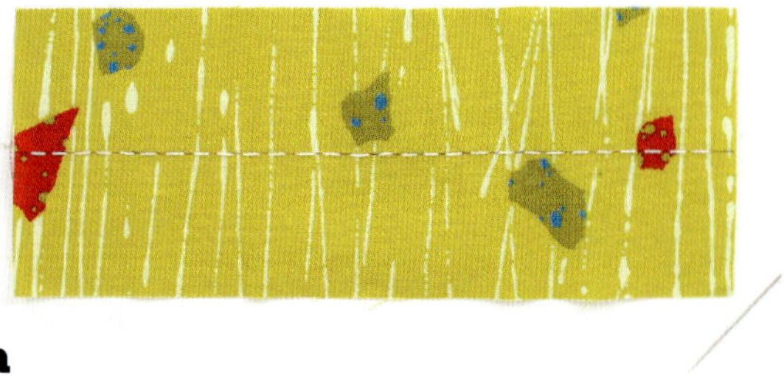

1a

1b

Prepare the Materials

Fuse piece H to the WS of piece A. Fuse piece J to the WS of piece B.

Hexies

1. Draw a line in the center of one 4″ × 12″ quilting cotton rectangle, then stitch over the line using the Patchwork Sashiko method (see Hand Stitching, page 28). Draw the next line on either side, ¼″ from the first line, then stitch over it. Repeat to stitch 5 lines on each side of the center line, a total of 11 lines. Repeat with the other 4 rectangles 4″ × 12″. Fuse the P44F to the WS of each stitched piece.
2. Position Hexagon Template 1 or the acrylic template equidistant from each other on the WS of the Step 1 rectangles, with 3 per rectangle. Repeat with the 8″ × 11″ Patchwork Sashiko textile, with 2 rows of 3, aligning two opposite points of each hexie on a stitch line. Trace around each template.
3. Cut out the hexie shapes. You need 6 Patchwork Sashiko hexies and 15 single layer fabric hexies.

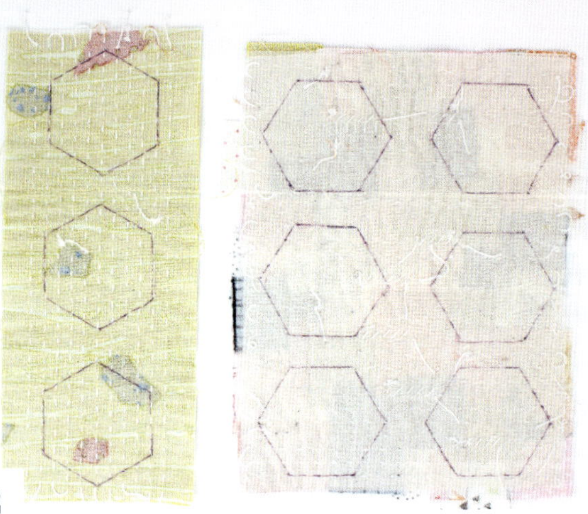

2

3a

3b

4

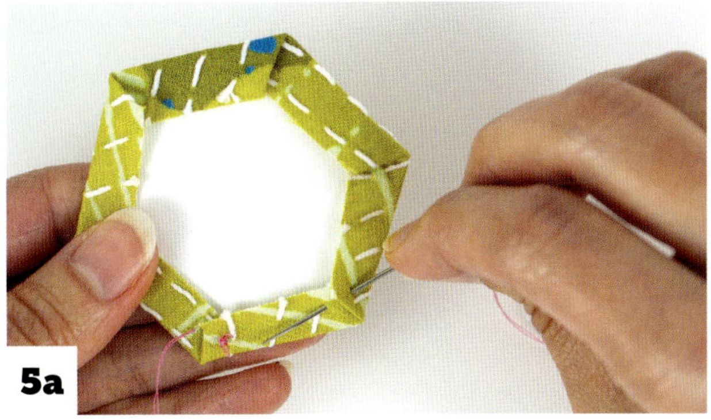
5a

4 Spritz the RS of the hexies with water before turning them over and placing the Hexagon Template 2 or purchased paper templates in the center. Fold the edges over the template, to the WS, and press one at a time. Flip to the RS, check the symmetry, and press again (steam, then dry).

5 Hand-sew the folds on all the hexies with a basting stitch. Cut a 32″ length of standard sewing machine thread, and thread the crewel needle. Pull the thread through so it's doubled (16″ in length), and knot the ends together. Insert the needle through both folds in one corner, then repeat at the next corner until all folds are stitched. At the last corner, make a knot.

5b

English Paper Piecing

Piecing the hexies together is the perfect craft for traveling. Once the hexies are basted, they can travel anywhere so you can stitch on the go. The diagram is just a suggestion, so feel free to lay them out however you'd like but with the same number of hexies per row.

1 Assign each single layer hexie fabric a number 1–5. Then, use the Hexie Layout Diagram to arrange the hexies. *PS* represents the Patchwork Sashiko hexies.

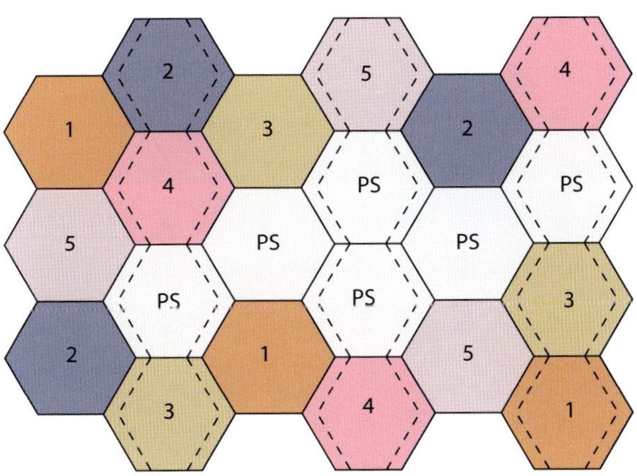

Hexie Layout Diagram

1

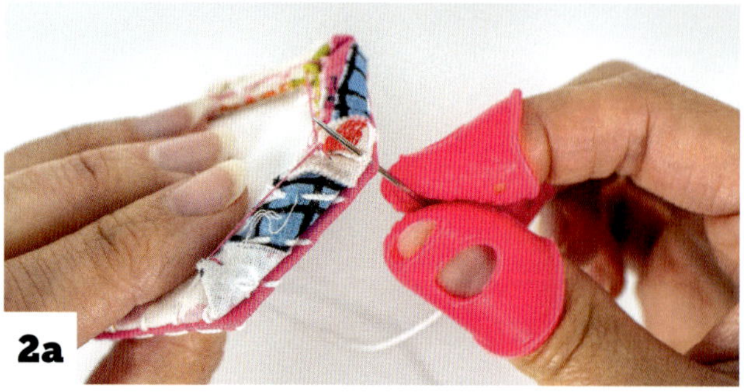

2a

2b

2c

3

2 Place 2 hexies RST. Thread the crewel needle with the crochet thread, knotting one end and leaving a 1½″ tail on the other. Stitch through the corners of the pieces, pull the thread through, then whipstitch the next stitch ³⁄₁₆″ away. Avoid hitting the paper template, stitching just the edge of the fold. It's okay if the stitches are visible from the right side. Continue until one side is stitched together. Don't knot the thread at the end.

3 Add the next hexie to the pair, RST, and repeat Step 2 to stitch them together.

4 Repeat Steps 2–3 to continue sewing all the hexies together. Sometimes, you will need to fold a hexie in half in order to sew the next edge. Knot and snip the thread when you run out of pieces that share an adjacent edge to the last piece you stitched. Then, start with a new thread.

4a

4b

5

1

5 Remove the hexie papers. Fuse piece I to the WS of the hexies (some pieces will be off the edge). Turn over and spritz the RS generously with water, then press 10–12 seconds with high dry heat.

Bag Assembly

Bag Body

1 Quilt prepared piece A with parallel straight lines ½″ apart, starting in the center of the piece. Draw the lines first or use a seam guide. Trim to 6½″ × 11″.

2 Quilt prepared piece B with 1″ diamonds. Draw an *X* through the square from corner to corner. Stitch over these lines. Then, draw and quilt parallel lines 1″ apart (or use a seam guide). Use Favorite Things Template 2 to cut out a circle.

3 Quilt the Patchwork Sashiko piece as indicated by the stitch lines in the Hexie Layout Diagram. Trim to 6½″ × 11″.

4 Place the Step 1 and Step 3 units RST, and sew together along the 2 short edges. Press the seam to the piece A side. Turn RS out, and topstitch along the seams.

2

3

4

5

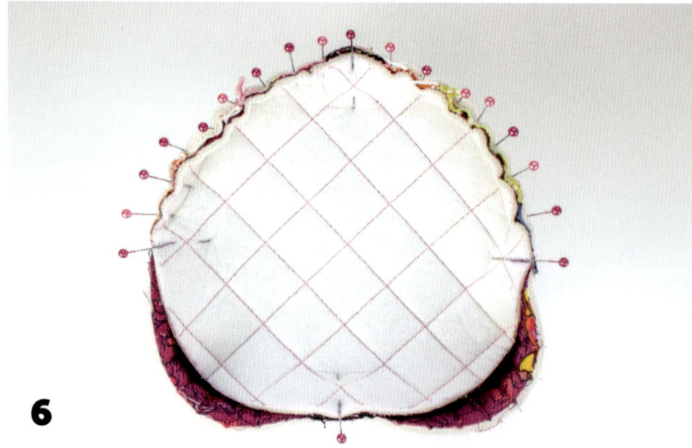

6

5 Draw a line down the center of each of the joined rectangles. Align the ends of the webbing on each line. Attach with a short line of stitches 1½″ from the top edge of the body (perpendicular to webbing). Then, sew from the stitched line to the bottom along both edges of the strap. Make sure not to sew the 2 rectangles together. Turn WS out.

6 Mark the Step 2 circle into quarters on the WS. Align these 4 points with the seams and straps, RST with the Step 5 unit. Pin at quarter marks. Then, pin around half of the circle, using a lot of pins.

7 Sew around the pinned curve, then pin and sew the other half of the circle.

7

Lining

1 Place the 2 E pieces RST, then sew the outer 1½″ of the straight edges together on both sides, leaving a gap in the center. Press the seam to either side.

2 Fold and press the 11″ edge of each D piece by ½″ twice. Topstitch close to the bottom fold.

1

3

4

3 To make the pockets, place a stitched D piece on top of each C piece, all RS up. Baste around the side and bottom edges of each pair. On 1 of the 2 pairs, sew down the center of the pocket, dividing it into two pockets.

4 Place the 2 units from Step 3 RST, and sew the two short edges together. Press the seam to one side, then turn RS out, and topstitch on that side.

5 Turn the lining piece WS out. Arrange the seams so they're in the center. Mark the 2 folds on the outer edges at the bottom.

6 Mark the lining bottom (from Step 1) into quarters on the WS. Then, RST, align and pin the lining and bottom at the 4 points. Pin around half of the circle, using a lot of pins. Sew around the pinned curve, then pin and sew the other half of the circle.

5

6a

6b

1a

1b

Drawstring Top

1. Fold and press the 2″ edges of both G pieces to the WS by ¼″ twice. Topstitch. Fold in half lengthwise, WST, and press. Mark the center point at the raw edge.
2. Lay 2 F pieces RS up. Mark the center point of the top edge. Align a G piece on each F piece, raw edges and center points aligned. Baste together with a long straight stitch along the top edge.
3. Place the 2 pieces from Step 2 RST, and sew the short ends together. Press the seams to one side, and topstitch.

2

3a

3b

4

5a

4 Place the remaining 2 F pieces RST, and sew together on the short edges. Press the seams in the same direction as the Step 3 unit, and topstitch.

5 Nest the Step 3 and Step 4 units together, RST and seams aligned. Sew around the top edge (the edge with the G casing pieces). Turn RS out. Press and topstitch the top edge.

5b

Final Assembly

1 With the exterior RS out, nest the drawstring top over the outside, raw edges aligned. The side of the drawstring top that will be the exterior of the bag should be touching the quilted exterior. Center the drawstring top side seams with the strap. Baste around the top edge.

// Line Things Up! // *The key to making sure all your bag layers get sewn together is to ensure all the raw edges are the same height. If the edges are uneven at the top, trim off the excess, then align. Make sure all layers are secured by the basting stitches.*

1

2a

2 Insert the Step 1 piece into the lining piece, RST. Match up the seams and top raw edges of the drawstring piece and the lining. Pin, and sew around the top.

3 Pull the bag through the opening in the lining. Stop when the lining is RS out. Press the raw edges of the gap in the lining to the WS, and sew the seam closed. Stuff the lining into the bag.

4 Stuff the drawstring top into the bag. Press the drawstring top around the top edge, and pin on the inside. Topstitch around the bottom of the drawstring top, just above the seam. Pull the drawstring top back out of the bag.

2b

3

4a

4b

5a

5 Insert a safety pin into the end of one of the ribbons, then feed it through one of the drawstring casings. Then, continue through the other casing.

6 Repeat Step 5 with the other ribbon, starting on the opposite side. There will be two ribbon ends on each side.

7 Tie a knot in each pair of ribbon tails. Trim the tails, then finish them. If the ribbon is made from a synthetic fiber, use a lighter to lightly sweep a flame over the ends, melting them. If the ribbon is a natural fiber, seal with fabric glue.

8 Press the bottom seam of the bag, smoothing and setting the structure.

5b

7

8

Early Harvest Apron

FINISHED SIZE: 26″ × 32″

Aprons are an everyday accessory in the kitchen for me. I'm a bit clumsy when baking, which means I'm also quite messy! The style of this apron is very comfortable because all the weight is distributed to the shoulders instead of the neck.

MATERIALS

- Scraps of quilting cotton in 3 different colors
- 1 yard medium-weight cotton (main fabric)
- 1 yard medium-weight cotton (for accent fabric)
- 3⅝ yards of 1″-wide cotton webbing (for straps)
- Crewel needle, size 2
- Cotton crochet thread, size 10 in white
- Apron Templates 1 and 2

CUTTING LIST

Access the required templates by going to Templates (page 46).

A: Cut 1 rectangle 28″ × 34″ from main fabric

B: Cut 1 Apron Template 2 from accent fabric

C: Cut 2 pieces 4½″ long from cotton webbing

D: Cut 2 pieces 59″ long from cotton webbing

Quilting Cotton Scraps

E: Cut 1 rectangle 2″ × 10″

F: Cut 1 rectangle 4″ × 7″

G: Cut 1 square 3″ × 3″

Apron Assembly

Prepare the Materials

Zigzag stitch the raw ends of each C and D piece of webbing.

Body

1 Lay piece A vertically, RS up. Place piece B on top, RS up, aligned to the bottom left corner. Pin in place. Topstitch with a zig-zag stitch around the curve (along the raw edge).

// Pinning is Winning // *When pinning large pieces together, I sometimes like to double pin to avoid shifting. Instead of inserting the pin through the fabric twice, I insert it 4 times.*

1

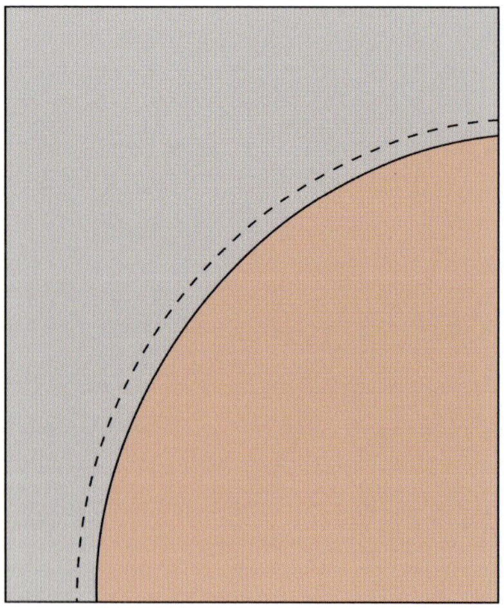

2

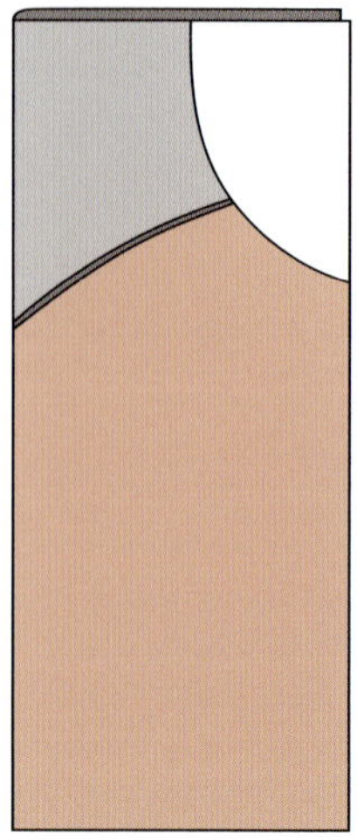

3a

3b

2 Cut away the excess piece A (main fabric) from the back side, leaving a 1″ around the curve. Fold over the raw edge of the main fabric to the WS, and press. Zigzag stitch around the curve of the main fabric only. Do not sew through the accent fabric.

3 Fold the unit in half, RST, so that the 34″ edges are aligned, and pin or clip. Align Template 1 with the upper right corner against the raw edges, and trace the curved edge. Cut along the traced line through both layers of the folded fabric.

KEEP THE CUT-OUTS! • *See that excess fabric remaining after cutting the curves out of the apron body? Those will be used for the pockets…isn't that great? So, keep them safe for the next section.*

4 Sew a 1″ seam along the two curves with a long straight basting stitch. Use the stitching as a guide to press the fabric to the WS on both curves. If necessary, snip into the curves so the fabric lies flat.

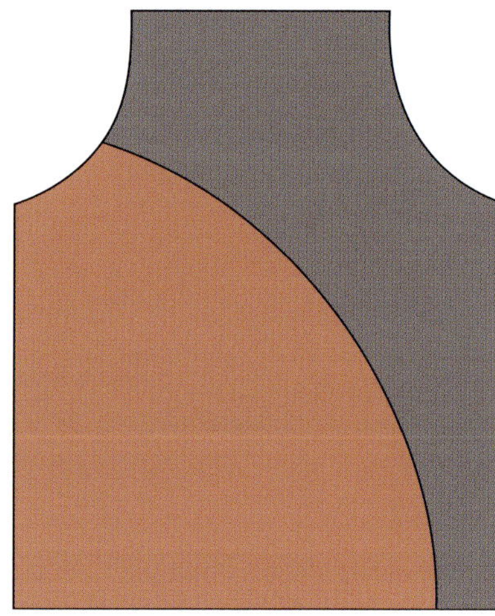

3c

4a

4b

5 Fold the raw edge under by ½″, and press. Sew around the curves with a ⅜″ seam allowance. Sew from the backside so you can see where the fold is. Remove the basting stitches if desired.

6 Fold all remaining straight edges to the WS by 1″, and press. Then, fold another ½″, tucking the raw edge under, and press. Topstitch along the folds that are closest to the center of the apron.

5

Pockets

1 Lay each pocket RS up. Mark or pin on the longest straight edge 3½″ from the right-angle corner, 5½″ from the same corner, and the center between these 2 points.

2 Fold the outer marks/pins to meet at the center mark/pin, creating a pleat. Pin in place. Sew over it with a basting stitch right along the edge.

1

2a

2b

3a

3b

3 With a long straight basting stitch, sew around the curved edge with a ½″ seam allowance. Use the stitching as a guide to press the fabric to the WS along the curve. If necessary, snip into the curve so it lies flat.

4 Fold the raw edge underneath the fold, and press. Pin. Topstitch around the curve on the WS, ¼″ away from the fold. Remove the basting stitches if desired.

5 Fold the short edge of the pocket to the WS by ¼″, and press. Fold another ¼″, concealing the raw edge, and press. Pin.

6 Repeat Step 5 on the long top edge. In order to keep the edge even with the pleats, fold the pleats all the way down to the curved edge, and pin in place. Then, trim the corner that meets the curve (as shown). Topstitch along the fold of the pleated edge only. Make 2 pockets.

4

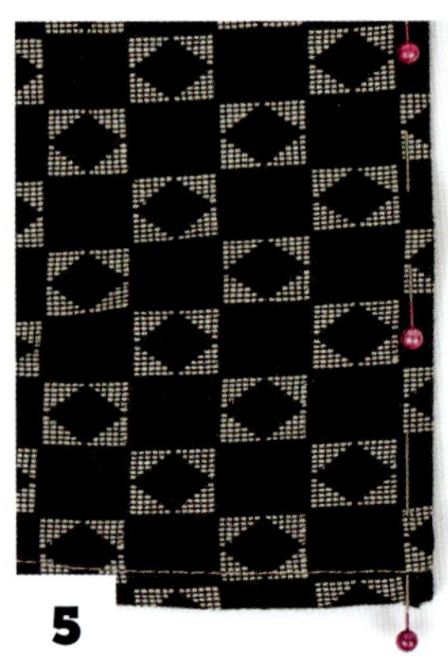

5

6a

6b

7 Position the pockets 17″ below the top edge of the apron and 3″ from the vertical center of the apron, on the RS. Fold the apron in half to mark the center line if needed. Pin in place, then topstitch around the short edge and bottom curved edge.

7

Straps and Loops

1 Fold the C pieces in half, and position them so they overlap the apron at the bottom of the arm curves (on the WS) with the fold 1″ past the edge. Pin in place. On the RS, draw an *X* where the webbing overlaps the fabric. Sew a box around the *X*, then sew the *X* on both loops.

2 Position one raw end of each D piece behind the upper corner of the arm curve on the WS, overlapping the fabric by 1″. Pin, then repeat Step 1 to sew a boxed *X* on both pieces.

1a

1b

2a

2b

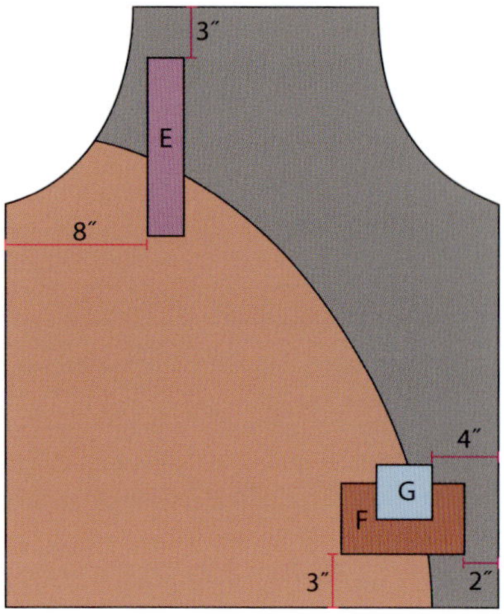

Apron Front Diagram

1

2

3

Patchwork Sashiko

1. Orient piece E using the Apron Front Layout Diagram. Pin in place. Draw lines across the length of the piece ¼″ apart, extending them past the short edges.
2. Use the Patchwork Sashiko method to hand stitch the drawn lines (see Hand Stitching, page 28), but don't leave any slack or loops.
3. Add more hand stitching perpendicular to the patchwork piece. Draw a line 6″ from the top of the patchwork piece. Then, add lines ¼″ apart over a 2″ span. Extend the lines 1″–1½″ past the left edge and 2″–3″ past the right edge of piece E. Repeat Step 2 to stitch them.

4

5

4 Orient piece F using the Apron Front Layout Diagram. Pin in place. Repeat Steps 1–2 to draw lines and hand stitch them.

5 Place piece G on top as shown in the Apron Front Layout Diagram. Pin in place. Repeat Steps 1–2 to draw lines and hand stitch them. Extend the lines above and below piece F.

6 To wear, insert the strap from each corner through the loop on the opposite side. Insert your head through the gap between the straps, then put your arms through the straps. Adjust the height to be what you want, then tie the straps at the back or front.

6

Saturday Market Crossbody Purse

FINISHED SIZE: 7″ × 10″ × 1½″

This crossbody purse is somewhere in between carrying everything you need for a trip and snagging just your wallet. Grab it for your everyday errands. The Patchwork Sashiko flap is front and center to show off your hard work.

MATERIALS

- 8″ × 10″ interfaced Patchwork Sashiko textile with stitching parallel to the long edges (for the flap)
- ⅓ yard quilting cotton (for bag exterior and loops)
- ⅓ yard quilting cotton (for lining)
- ¼ yard Bosal In-R-Form Single Sided Fusible Foam
- 1⅝ yards of 1″-wide cotton or polyester webbing
- 2 D-Rings, size 1″
- 2 swivel clasps, size 1″
- Adjustable slide buckle, size 1″
- 1 set magnetic sew-in snaps (from By Annie)
- Pinking shears
- Lighter or fabric glue (optional)
- Crossbody Templates 1 and 2

CUTTING LIST

Access the required templates by going to Templates (page 46). Prepare the templates by printing them, and then cutting them out of the paper.

Exterior Fabric

From the exterior fabric:

A: Cut 2 Template 1

B: Cut 1 rectangle 2″ × 23½″

C: Cut 2 rectangles 2″ × 2½″

Lining Fabric

From the lining fabric:

D: Cut 2 Template 1

E: Cut 1 rectangle 2″ × 23½″

F: Cut 1 Template 2

G: Cut 1 Template 2 from the Patchwork Sashiko textile

Foam

From the Bosal foam:

H: Cut 2 Template 1

I: Cut 1 rectangle 2″ × 23½″

J: Cut 1 Template 2

CITRUS
ROSEMARY
Sweet Fig jam
CITRUS
ROSEMARY
Sweet Fig jam

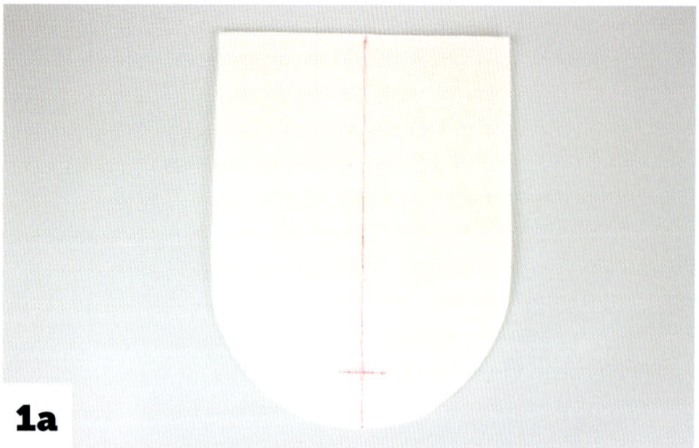

1a

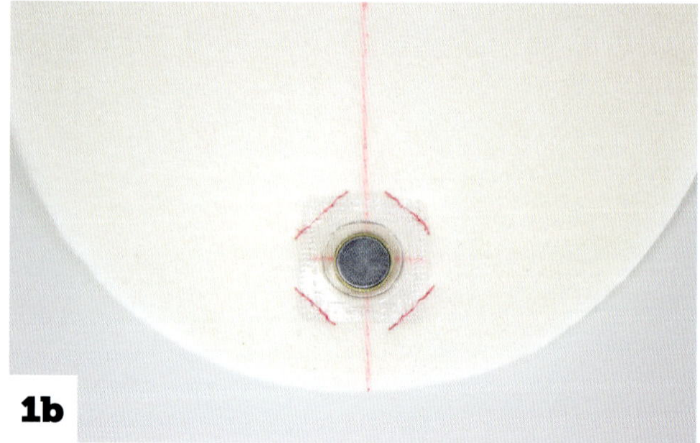

1b

Prepare the Materials

1. Mark piece J down the center (fold in half and mark on the non-fusible side). Mark on the line 1¼″ up from the bottom curve. Place the magnetic snap on the line intersection, **magnetic side up**. Sew diagonally across the plastic corners by moving the needle all the way to the left, making sure the foot can clear the edge of the magnet.
2. Fuse piece J to the WS of piece G.
3. Repeat Step 1 with 1 piece H, making the second mark 3½″ down from the top of the edge. Sew the other half of the magnetic snap on the mark, **magnetic side down**.
4. Fuse the 2 H pieces onto the WS of the A pieces.

DON'T TRUST FUSIBLE FOAM? • *Sometimes, fusible foam can detach from the fabric over time if not fused well. If you're worried about this, apply some light quilting to the A/H and J/G fused units, being careful to avoid the magnetic snaps.*

5. Fuse piece I to the WS of piece B.
6. Trim the webbing to 55″ long. If the webbing is made from a synthetic fiber, use a lighter to lightly sweep a flame over the ends, melting them. If the webbing is a natural fiber, seal with fabric glue.

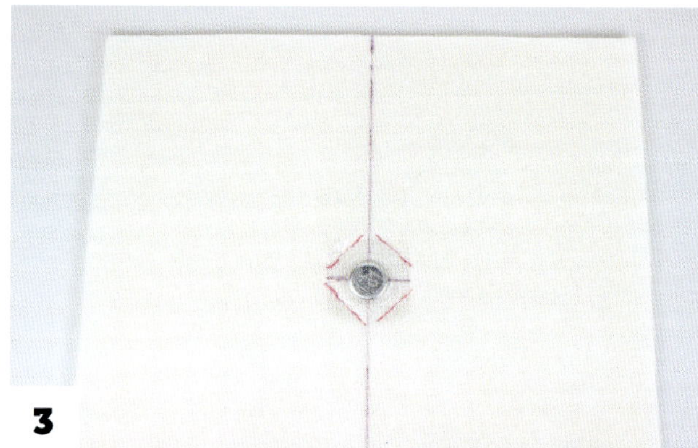

3

1

2

Body and Lining

1. Fold both A pieces and piece B in half (RST), and mark the center of the bottom edges with a pin.
2. Match up the centers of one A piece and the B piece, RST. Sew 5″ along the bottom, starting and stopping right before the curved corners.

3a

3b

3 Align one end of piece B with the top of the A piece, RST. Pin once at the top first to make sure the edges match, then add more pins along the side and curve. Sew. Repeat on the other side.

4 Repeat Steps 2–3 to add the second A piece on top, sandwiching the B piece and aligning all right sides. Turn the unit RS out.

5 Repeat Steps 1–4 with pieces D and E. During Step 2, only sew ½″ on each bottom edge, leaving a 4″ gap in the bottom. Keep the gap pinned while you sew so piece E stays in place.

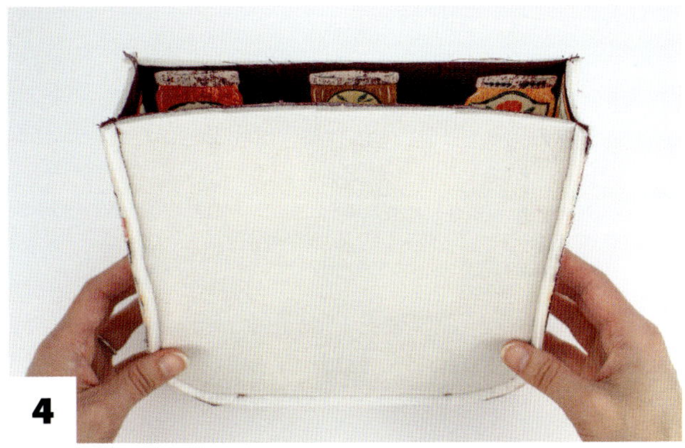
4

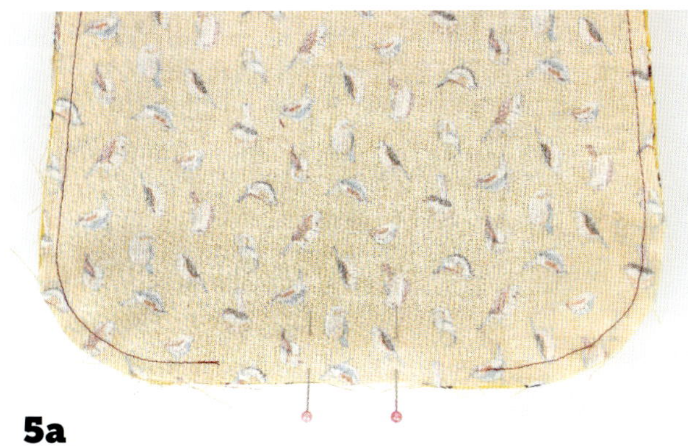
5a

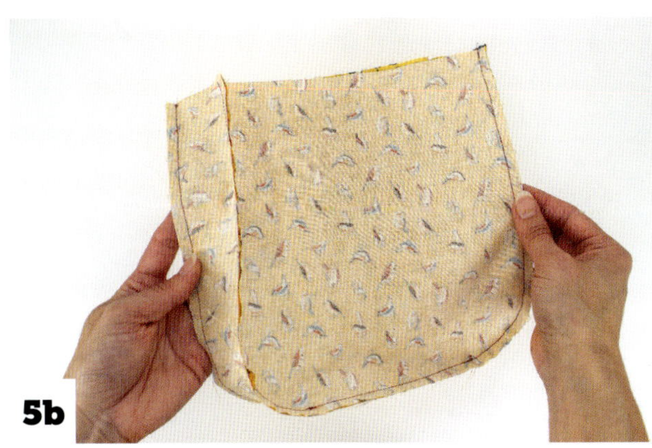
5b

1

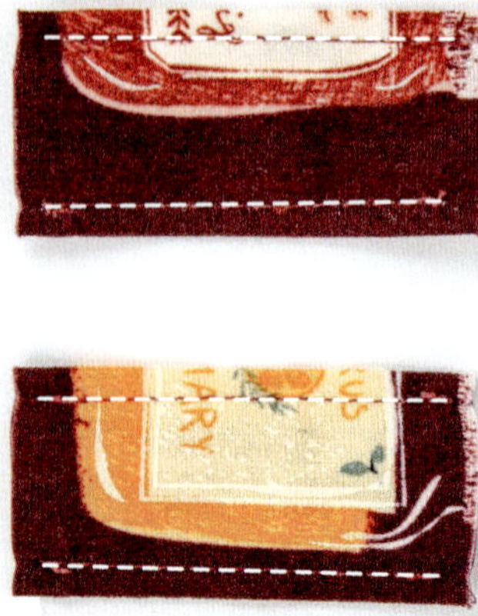

2

3

Loops

1. Fold the C pieces in half, RST and matching short edges. Sew the short edges together.
2. Turn the loops RS out, then fold and press so the seams are in the center. Topstitch the 2 folded edges.
3. Fold the units in half again, with raw edges together and the seam on the inside. Press. Insert through the D-rings, aligning the raw edges. Sew a line across the loop as close to the D-ring as possible.
4. Align the raw edges of the D-ring loops to the top raw edge of the bag exterior, centered on the B piece on each side (RST). Baste in place with a long straight stitch.

4

Flap

1. Align pieces G and F, RST. Sew together around the curve, leaving the straight edge open. Use pinking shears to trim around the curve.
2. Turn the flap RS out, and press. Topstitch around the edge. Baste the straight side closed with a long straight stitch.

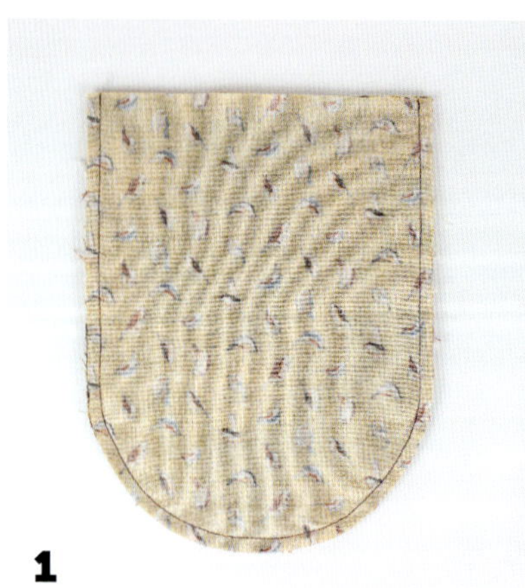

1

2

1

2

3

Strap

1 Insert one end of the webbing through a swivel clasp. Pull through 1″ and fold over. Sew a line of stitches as close to the edge of the clasp as possible, then a second line of stitching as close to the webbing end as possible. The side with the visible end is the WS.

2 Insert the other end of the webbing through the slide buckle. Slide the buckle about 12″ onto the webbing. Make sure the center bar of the buckle is visible on the WS.

3 Insert the same end from Step 2 through the second swivel clasp. Make sure the clasp is on the RS as shown.

4 Create some slack in the webbing where it passes over the slide buckle. Insert the same webbing end from Step 3 back through the slide buckle. Pull through 1″. Fold the raw end over to the WS. Audition the position of the slide, clasp, and fold to ensure they are correctly oriented.

5 With as much slack as you need to comfortably sew, sew the end of the webbing to itself as shown, making a closed loop. Sew 1 line of stitches as close to the buckle as possible, and another as close to the end of the webbing as possible.

4

5a

5b

1

Final Assembly

1. On the bag exterior back (the side without the snap), center the flap front RST to the top edge. Pin and baste together.
2. Stuff the exterior into the lining, RST and aligning the top edges. Make sure the seams of the body and lining match. Pin at the seams, then pin around the whole top. Sew around the top edge.
3. Reach through the gap in the lining and pull the exterior through, leaving the lining sticking out of the body.
4. Press the raw edges of the gap to the WS, then sew the gap closed. Stuff the lining into the body.

2

3

4

5a

5b

5. Press the top edge of the bag so the lining wraps over the top edge (with the flap open and away from the bag). Fold the D-ring loops up. Press the seam at the bottom of the flap on the lining side so that the seam aligns with the top of the bag. Pin, and topstitch making sure to sew the D-ring loops upward.
6. Fold the flap so the snaps click together. Pull up on the flap and fold it so there is no slack, and clip together. Press that fold, and draw a line across the flap ¾″ below the fold. Make sure the line looks straight and even. Sew over the line through both flap layers.
7. Attach the swivel clasps of the strap to the D-rings.

6a

6b

7

Slow Sunday Sandals

FINISHED SIZE: Women's shoe size 6 to 14; Men's shoe size 4½ to 12½

We don't wear shoes inside the house, so there are a variety of indoor sandals and slippers strategically placed around the home. This playful, patterned pair is a favorite!

MATERIALS

- 10″ × 12″ interfaced Patchwork Sashiko textile (for strap exterior)
- Fat quarter of quilting cotton (for sole and strap lining)
- ⅓ yard of duck canvas, denim, or anti-skid gripper fabric (for bottom)
- ¼ yard of Bosal In-R-Form Single Sided Fusible Foam (for sole and strap)
- ¼ yard of Pellon 70 Peltex
- ¾ yard of quilting cotton for bias binding
- Sandal Templates 1 and 2

CUTTING LIST

Access the required templates by going to Templates (page 46). Prepare the templates by printing them, and then cutting them out of the paper. Template 2 includes US women's sizes 6–14 and US men's sizes 4.5–12.5. Trace both A pieces (mirrored) onto the Patchwork Sashiko textile before cutting either out to make sure they both fit.

A: Cut 2 Template 1 (mirrored) from the Patchwork Sashiko textile

B: Cut 2 Template 2 (mirrored) from the bottom fabric

C: Cut 2 Template 1 (mirrored) from the lining fabric

D: Cut 2 Template 2 (mirrored) from the sole fabric

E: Cut 2 Template 1 (mirrored) from the Bosal foam

F: Cut 2 Template 2 (mirrored) from the Bosal foam

G: Cut 2 Template 2 from the Peltex

Bias Binding:

Cut 2 strips 2¼″-wide diagonally across the fabric. Trim the strip ends straight. (Reserve the extra for another use.)

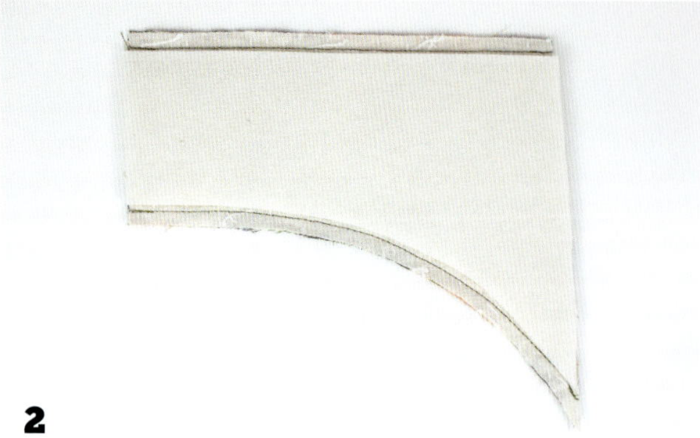

2

3

Strap

1 Trim away ⅜″ of the curved bottom and straight top edge of both E pieces. Fuse the E pieces to the WS of the A pieces, making sure the A pieces extend past the trimmed E pieces equally. Fuse from the textile side.

2 Layer with the C pieces, RST. Pin, then sew along the curve and across the top edge, not sewing through the foam on both units.

3 Turn the pieces RS out. Baste the remaining open edges closed with a long straight stitch. Trim the excess seam allowance at the tips.

Sole

1 Fuse the F pieces to the WS of the D pieces. Quilt them together with diagonal lines 1″ apart, or as desired. Draw lines before quilting or use a seam guide.

2 Place the B pieces WS up. Place the G pieces on top, aligning the shapes. Place the Step 1 units on top, RS facing up. Pin, then baste around the whole edge.

1

2

Assembly

Repeat Steps 1–3 for both sandals.

1 Mark 1¾″ down from the top of each sole. Layer the strap on top as shown. Pin the short side to the sole, parallel to the edge.

1

2

3a

2 Place your foot in the sandal, and adjust the loose side of the strap to the sole until it feels comfortable. Pin in place on the edge of the sole, aligning the wide side of the strap down the sole as needed. Then, try walking in the sandal. Make sure the strap is not too tight or too loose, and adjust as needed.

3 Flip the sandals over and trim away the excess strap. Baste the straps to the edges of the sole on both sides.

3b

Finish The Sandals

Repeat Steps 2–6 for both sandals.

1 Fold each piece of bias binding lengthwise, WS together, and pin every 2″.

2 Leaving 5″ of excess binding at the start, sew the binding to the bottom edge of the sole, starting where the top of the long edge of the strap meets the edge of the sole. Sew around the sole, then stop where the bottom edge of the strap meets the edge of the sole (there will be excess binding).

1

2

3a

3b

3 Pin the 5″ tail to the sole, lay the other tail on top, and draw a line (or insert a pin) where the bottom tail stops. Measure 2¼″ from that mark toward the end of the top tail and cut the top tail.

4 Remove all pins. Unfold the upper tail. On the WS, draw a line 2¼″ from the end, and then a diagonal line from corner to corner. Fold the sole in half with the bottoms together, and pin or clip in place. Position the upper tail (5″ tail) on top of the other tail, RST and at a right angle. Pin together. Then, sew over the diagonal line.

4a

4b

4c

5a

5b

6a

5 Trim the excess fabric to ¼″, and press open. Refold the binding, and finish sewing it to the bottom of the sole.

6 Turn over to the front side, and fold the binding over the top edge. Topstitch along the fold with a ¼″ presser foot, using a stiletto as needed. The binding should just cover the stitch line from Steps 2 and 5.

6b

Comfy Cafe Curtains

FINISHED SIZE: 2 Curtains 23″ × 18″

I love cafe curtains. They provide privacy from looky-loos but still let all the beautiful sunlight in! These curtains would be perfect hanging in the kitchen or in a home office. Just enough hand stitching to add interest and a bold color block design. French seams give a professional finish.

MATERIALS

- ¼ yard each of 3 cotton woven fabrics (Fabrics 1, 3, and 4)
- ⅜ yard of 1 cotton woven fabric (Fabric 2)
- Crewel needle, size 2
- Cotton crochet thread, size 10 in white
- 24″ curtain rod (optional, to fit window)
- Curtain clips (optional, for hanging)

Material Notes

Fabrics must have a usable width of 42″. If using striped fabrics, purchase ¾ yard to make vertical stripes. I used Fabric 2 twice in each curtain.

CUTTING LIST

A: Cut 2 rectangles 7″ × 21″ from Fabric 1

B: Cut 2 rectangles 4″ × 21″ from Fabric 2

C: Cut 2 rectangles 8″ × 21″ from Fabric 2

D: Cut 2 rectangles 4″ × 21″ from Fabric 3

E: Cut 2 rectangles 6″ × 21″ from Fabric 4

Panel Assembly

The two 18″ × 24″ curtains are mirror images of each other. Refer to the diagram for piecing layout, and reverse/mirror the diagram to piece the second curtain.

1. Place 2 panels **WST**, aligning edges. Pin together. Sew with a ¼″ seam.
2. Trim away half of the seam allowance.

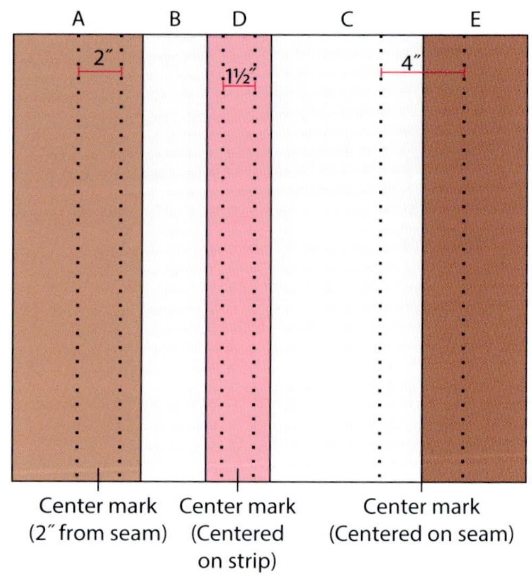

Panel Piecing and Stitching Diagram

3a

3b

3. Fold and press the panels **RST**. Sew together again, using a ¼″ seam.
4. Repeat to piece together all the panels according to the diagram.
5. Press all the seams away from pieces B and C. Topstitch all the seams. Repeat to make the second curtain.

4

5

Patchwork Sashiko

1. Use the diagram to locate and mark the center point of each hand-stitched area. Mark the right and left boundaries of each area of hand stitching. Starting in the center, draw lines in the stitching areas across the whole curtain. The lines should be ½″ apart.

1

2 Hand stitch over all the lines using the Patchwork Sashiko method (see Hand Stitching, page 28). Increase the stitch length to between ⅜″ and ½″. Don't leave slack or loops, and don't stitch over a line that falls directly on a seam. Use a 20″ piece of thread so that each line uses its own piece.

// Load it Up! // *Stitching through one layer of fabric is much easier than multiple layers. Try to load up as many folds of fabric as you can.*

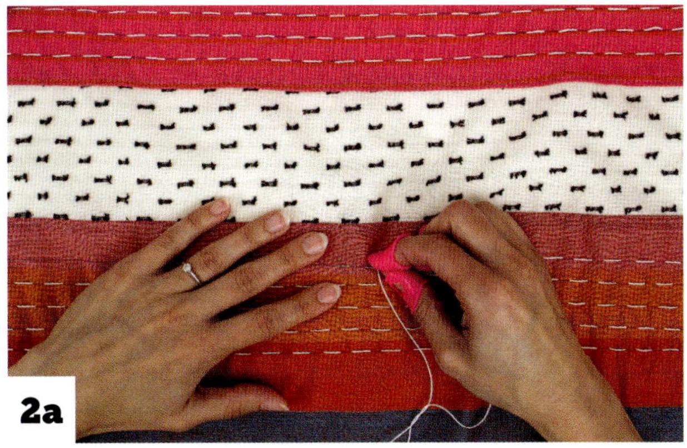

2a

2b

Finish

1 Trim the top and bottom edges of each curtain to straighten them, trimming no more than ¼″.

2 Hem the bottom of each curtain. Press the raw edge to the WS by ⅜″, and then again by ⅜″ to conceal the raw edge. Topstitch.

3 Repeat Step 2 to hem the sides of each curtain.

4 Hem the top of each curtain. Press the raw edge to the WS by ½″, then again by 1½″ to conceal the raw edge. Topstitch the bottom fold from the WS, forming a casing for a curtain rod.

2

4

ABOUT THE AUTHOR

DIANA LI FITZGERALD grew up in a family of creatives, continuing the traditions of her seamstress grandmother and sewist/fiber artist/sculptor mother. Her former career in science fed her analytical tendencies, and once she found sewing, she realized it was the perfect unity of experimentation and creativity, complementing her technical side. She currently designs sewing patterns, teaches, and tinkers with different sewing and hand stitching techniques full-time. Her patterns, workshops and lectures have been featured on the national stage in person and also offered online. She loves discovering new ideas and finding creative solutions to problems. Sewing, thankfully, has no end to either.

Visit Diana online and follow on social media!

Website: banjoflannel.com
Blog: banjoflannel.com/blog
Instagram: @banjoflannel
Facebook: /banjoflannel
Pinterest: /banjoflannel
YouTube: /banjoflannel